New Directions for Community Colleges

Arthur M. Cohen
EDITOR-IN-CHIEF

Florence B. Brawer
Richard L. Wagoner
ASSOCIATE EDITORS

Carrie B. Kisker
Edward Francis Ryan
MANAGING EDITORS

The Current Landscape and Changing Perspectives of Part-Time Faculty

Richard L. Wagoner
EDITOR

Number 140 • Winter 2007
Jossey-Bass
San Francisco

THE CURRENT LANDSCAPE AND CHANGING PERSPECTIVES OF PART-TIME FACULTY
Richard L. Wagoner (ed.)
New Directions for Community Colleges, no. 140

Arthur M. Cohen, Editor-in-Chief
Florence B. Brawer, Richard L. Wagoner, Associate Editors

NEW DIRECTIONS FOR COMMUNITY COLLEGES (ISSN 0194-3081, electronic ISSN 1536-0733) is part of The Jossey-Bass Higher and Adult Education Series and is published quarterly by Wiley Subscription Services, Inc., A Wiley Company, at Jossey-Bass, 989 Market Street, San Francisco, California 94103-1741. Periodicals Postage Paid at San Francisco, California, and at additional mailing offices. POSTMASTER: Send address changes to New Directions for Community Colleges, Jossey-Bass, 989 Market Street, San Francisco, California 94103-1741.

SUBSCRIPTIONS cost $85.00 for individuals and $209.00 for institutions, agencies, and libraries in the United States. Prices subject to change. See order form at the back of book.

EDITORIAL CORRESPONDENCE should be sent to the Editor-in-Chief, Arthur M. Cohen, at the Graduate School of Education and Information Studies, University of California, Box 951521, Los Angeles, California 90095-1521. All manuscripts receive anonymous reviews by external referees.

New Directions for Community Colleges is indexed in CIJE: Current Index to Journals in Education (ERIC), Contents Pages in Education (T&F), Current Abstracts (EBSCO), Ed/Net (Simpson Communications), Education Index/Abstracts (H.W. Wilson), Educational Research Abstracts Online (T&F), ERIC Database (Education Resources Information Center), and Resources in Education (ERIC).

Microfilm copies of issues and articles are available in 16mm and 35mm, as well as microfiche in 105mm, through University Microfilms Inc., 300 North Zeeb Road, Ann Arbor, Michigan 48106-1346.

CONTENTS

EDITOR'S NOTES

Part-time faculty have been a prominent presence in community colleges for several decades. As a result, scholars and educators have spent much time debating the advantages and disadvantages of a part-time academic workforce, comparing part-timers to their full-time counterparts, and studying the part-time faculty experience. Since the 1990s, however, more part-time than full-time faculty have been employed in community colleges. In 2003, part-timers made up 66.7 percent of the public two-year academic workforce (U.S. Department of Education, 2005). Besides for-profit colleges, the community college is the only type of postsecondary institution in the United States where part-time faculty outnumber full-time faculty on many campuses. This fact has significant implications for community college administrators who are responsible for recruiting, hiring, and supporting part-time faculty; for college, district, and state leaders who help set policies regarding the use of part-timers; and for all part-time faculty who seek to receive equitable treatment as they strive to enhance the quality of education for community college students.

Although part-time faculty make up the majority of the community college academic labor force, *New Directions for Community Colleges* has not dedicated a complete issue to the topic since 1980 (Parsons, 1980). Since then, few of the notions introduced in that volume have been questioned. Most important, the financial benefits of a part-time workforce—mentioned as one reason for the use of part-timers in 1980—has become the predominant justification that administrators use today (Wagoner, Metcalfe, and Olaore, 2005). While constant budget pressures force community colleges to employ large numbers of part-time faculty, potentially negative effects of such practices—including diminished instructional quality, the challenges of managing a predominantly temporary labor force, and the difficulties in supporting oneself on a part-time instructor's salary—must also be considered. It is therefore necessary to reexamine the conceptions, practices, and perspectives related to the employment of part-time faculty in community colleges in the twenty-first century.

Drawing on nationally representative quantitative data from the 1988, 1993, 1999, and the newly released 2004 National Study of Postsecondary Faculty (NSOPF), qualitative fieldwork, and the experiences of administrators and faculty members, this volume provides a variety of perspectives on part-time community college faculty. In Chapter One, Kevin Eagan presents an aggregated national portrait of part-time faculty based on his analysis of the NSOPF data. He suggests that a stasis of sorts has been reached nationally

in the use of part-timers. As Eagan notes, his findings complement earlier studies, which is perhaps the ideal starting point for this volume, as it seeks to present an accurate picture of the part-time labor force while simultaneously questioning some of the accepted conceptions of them.

Chapters Two and Three begin the questioning process. John S. Levin suggests in Chapter Two how part-time faculty can be understood as extensions of institutional identity of twenty-first-century colleges and offers a cogent challenge at the end of the chapter, indicating that to change the current practices regarding part-time faculty, individuals must be willing to challenge the missions and goals of modern community colleges. Moving from this institutional perspective, my findings in Chapter Three present a conceptualization of part-time faculty as a new economy labor force. Central to this conceptualization is the need to disaggregate part-time faculty in order to better understand and interpret their use. These two chapters, then, question dominant conceptions of part-time faculty and present different ways of thinking about part-timers that are better aligned with their current roles in community colleges based on colleges' purposes today.

Grounding the discourse in practical concerns, Donald W. Green presents one senior administrator's view and experience in Chapter Four. He addresses the issues of finding, hiring, orienting, evaluating, and developing adjuncts, with an emphasis on ensuring quality and maintaining institutional standards. Often part-time faculty are not allowed a voice in scholarly discussions about their positions in community colleges; this volume includes two chapters dedicated to this perspective as a partial remedy to this lack of inclusion. Written by Robert B. Yoshioka, Chapter Five presents in strong terms the dissatisfaction and frustration that some part-time faculty members can feel. This chapter also describes how the Internet and e-mail have facilitated the organization of part-time faculty groups like the California Part-Time Faculty Association (CPFA). As indicated in the chapter, these groups allow part-timers to act collectively to seek improvements in their positions. CPFA chose to support and endorse legislation that will change policy affecting part-time faculty in California. To this point, the CPFA's efforts have produced mixed results, but they indicate one method that part-timers can use to work beyond their campuses to seek change. The Washington Part-Time Faculty Association, Eddy A. Ruiz's focus in Chapter Seven, has chosen a different method to implement change: litigation. Ruiz summarizes the lawsuits brought against the state of Washington and its community colleges and the implications these cases might have nationally.

Chapters Seven and Eight revisit the themes discussed in Chapter Four. Vernon C. Smith, in Chapter Seven, presents the systems approach employed by Rio Salado College in Arizona, demonstrating best practices that help increase effectiveness and suggesting that a college's orientation to the globalized new economy does not necessarily guarantee instability and exploitation of part-time faculty. Chapter Eight increases the breadth and depth of effective policies and practices with Desna L. Wallin's exploration of programs dedicated to the professional development of part-time faculty at three community colleges that have proven effective in increasing part-time faculty integration. Returning to one of the themes of the opening chapter, I explore part-time faculty satisfaction in Chapter Nine. The chapter's analysis of the 1999 NSOPF data set indicates that disaggregating faculty groups offered a more nuanced perspective of faculty satisfaction than that of an aggregate view. While on the whole, part-time faculty might be described as satisfied, faculty associated with the different purposes of colleges and with different disciplines have significantly different levels of satisfaction.

The multiple perspectives presented in this volume offer a complex and conflicted picture of community college part-time faculty, as there are no easy answers to the questions that arise from colleges' heavy reliance on their service. As editor, I sought to solicit chapters that would encourage discussion and debate on the topic to update and advance the scholarship on part-time faculty while also highlighting best practices and useful examples that can help the two-year college continue to play a vital role in American higher education.

Richard L. Wagoner
Editor

References

Parsons, M. H. (ed.). *Using Part-Time Faculty Effectively*. New Directions for Community Colleges, no. 30. San Francisco: Jossey-Bass, 1980.

U.S. Department of Education. *National Study of Postsecondary Faculty (NSOPF: 04): Report on Faculty and Instructional Staff in Fall 2003*. Washington, D.C.: U.S. Department of Education, 2005.

Wagoner, R. L., Metcalfe, A. S., and Olaore, I. "Fiscal Reality and Academic Quality: Part-Time Faculty and the Challenge to Organizational Culture at Community Colleges." *Community College Journal of Research and Practice*, 2005, 29, 1–20.

RICHARD L. WAGONER *is assistant professor of higher education and organizational change in the Graduate School of Education and Information Studies at the University of California, Los Angeles.*

1

This chapter provides a descriptive analysis of the demographic, employment, and attitudinal similarities and differences found among part- and full-time faculty at community colleges.

A National Picture of Part-Time Community College Faculty: Changing Trends in Demographics and Employment Characteristics

Kevin Eagan

The employment of part-time faculty at community colleges across the United States has increased steadily since the early 1970s (Cohen and Brawer, 2003). In the fall of 2003, part-time faculty comprised 67 percent of community college faculty by head count (Cataldi, Fahimi, Bradburn, and Zimbler, 2005). In part, community colleges have employed part-time faculty because they are inexpensive to hire, have expertise in highly specialized areas such as vocational training, and provide the college with some flexibility (Cohen and Brawer, 2003; Rhoades, 1996).

Although part-time faculty continue to dominate the instructional workforce of community colleges, relatively little is known about this diverse group of individuals. Leslie and Gappa (2002) suggest that the media popularize stereotypes and assumptions about part-time community college faculty that often do not apply to the majority of individuals working in these appointments. Part-timers are often portrayed as being "free-way flyers" who constantly seek full-time appointments in postsecondary education institutions. However, as this chapter demonstrates, only a small proportion of part-time faculty have more than one academic appointment at a postsecondary education institution. Instead, the majority of part-time faculty tend to come from full-time jobs in other professional fields and

NEW DIRECTIONS FOR COMMUNITY COLLEGES, no. 140, Winter 2007 © 2007 Wiley Periodicals, Inc.
Published online in Wiley InterScience (www.interscience.wiley.com) • DOI: 10.1002/cc.299

pursue part-time academic opportunities because of an interest and satisfaction in teaching (Cohen and Brawer, 2003; Gappa and Leslie, 1997).

Considering that the number of part-time faculty is growing, it is important to explore the composition of this significant segment of the postsecondary labor force. Drawing from the four most recent administrations of the National Study of Postsecondary Faculty (NSOPF), this chapter illustrates trends in the composition of part-time community college faculty as well as changes in their attitudes and beliefs across time. In addition, this chapter provides a descriptive analysis of the demographic, employment, and attitudinal similarities and differences found among part- and full-time faculty at community colleges.

Methods

This chapter uses data from the 1988, 1993, 1999, and 2004 administrations of the NSOPF. Each survey administration randomly sampled part- and full-time faculty in postsecondary education institutions. Because of the sampling strategies and weighting methods associated with the surveys, descriptive statistics reported in this chapter represent national norms. Heuer and others (2006) provide technical and methodological information regarding sampling, weighting, and measurement error for the 2004 NSOPF.

Demographic Characteristics

Table 1.1 presents demographic characteristics of full- and part-time faculty between 1988 and 2004. Results over time demonstrate gender parity between full-time and part-time faculty. In the late 1980s and early 1990s, men represented the majority in both part- and full-time faculty appointments at community colleges. In the 2004 NSOPF, women and men had essentially equal representation in community college faculty appointments.

As gender differences between part-time and full-time faculty have disappeared, racial disparities have persisted. A higher proportion of part-time faculty identify as white compared to their full-time colleagues. In contrast, a small but increasing trend has seen a larger percentage of full-time faculty identifying as Asian or Asian American compared to their part-time counterparts. Nonetheless, the overall picture of community college faculty does not reflect an image of diversity. The trend in the past twenty years has featured more nonwhite individuals assuming faculty appointments at community colleges; however, faculty identifying as white still represent more than 82 percent of all community college faculty.

Small differences also exist between part-timers and full-timers in regard to age, as contingent faculty are more likely to be younger compared to their full-time counterparts. The 2004 NSOPF survey, however, suggests no significant age difference: the average age of part-time faculty is 49.2 years versus 49.8 years for full-time faculty.

NEW DIRECTIONS FOR COMMUNITY COLLEGES • DOI: 10.1002/cc

Table 1.1. Demographic Characteristics of Part- and Full-Time Faculty

	Part-Time Faculty				Full-Time Faculty			
	1988	1993	1999	2004	1988	1993	1999	2004
Gender								
Male	60.0	53.4	50.7	50.8	62.1	53.8	48.9	50.7
Female	40.0	46.6	49.3	49.2	37.9	46.2	51.1	49.3
Race								
White	91.4	88.1	86.2	83.8	90.6	85.9	84.9	81.4
Black	3.0	4.6	5.8	7.0	3.3	6.4	6.3	7.2
Hispanic	3.4	4.1	4.8	4.3	3.6	3.7	4.6	5.5
Asian	1.7	2.4	2.1	2.9	1.7	3.0	3.5	4.3
American Indian	0.6	0.8	1.0	1.9	0.9	0.9	0.7	1.7
Degree								
Doctoral	7.8	7.4	7.8	8.6	17.7	16.6	18.0	17.9
Professional	5.2	5.0	2.5	3.7	1.7	2.3	1.8	1.5
Master's	47.2	52.2	56.3	51.4	64.0	64.2	61.4	62.3
Bachelor's	28.8	25.6	21.9	21.9	12.8	12.0	13.3	11.6
Less than Bachelor's degree	11.0	9.9	11.5	14.4	3.9	4.9	5.5	6.7
Average age	44.0	45.6	47.7	49.2	47.3	48.3	49.4	49.8

When considering educational attainment, differences between part-time and full-time faculty become readily apparent. The data suggest that full-time faculty generally have obtained higher degrees than their part-time colleagues. The proportion of full-time community college faculty holding a doctorate is consistently more than twice that of part-time faculty, and full-time faculty are also more likely than part-timers to have earned a master's degree. In contrast, part-time faculty are significantly more likely to hold professional degrees than their full-time counterparts. The differences in educational attainment suggest different career paths for part-time and full-time faculty. Although a number of individuals employed in part-time instructional positions at community colleges are pursuing graduate education simultaneously, other part-timers work in other professional fields, such as business and technology, where the doctorate is not required (Cohen and Brawer, 2003). In contrast, full-time faculty likely have sought to make academia their career and thus have pursued and obtained more advanced training in their field. Haeger (1998) suggests that less education among part-time faculty threatens the level of quality in academic programs; however, studies have not found significant differences in instructional quality between full-time and part-time faculty (Cohen and Brawer, 2003; Grubb, 1999).

Employment Characteristics

Table 1.2 presents results from descriptive analyses of employment characteristics of full- and part-time faculty. Not surprisingly, the vast majority of
both part-time and full-time faculty identify teaching as the principal activity for their position. Over time, 93 percent of part-time faculty indicate that
teaching is their primary responsibility at the institution, while an average
of 83 percent of full-time faculty do so. Full-time faculty who do not identify teaching as their principal activity tend to serve administrative roles at
their respective institutions. Finally, the survey respondents reaffirm the
notion that research is not central to the community college mission: less
than 0.5 percent list research as the principal activity of their position.

The four NSOPF administrations suggest that a greater proportion of
part-time faculty teach in the arts and humanities, while a larger percentage
of full-time faculty assume instructional roles in science and engineering.
Over time, the proportion of part-time faculty in education and social sciences has increased, while the percentage of full-timers in these fields has
remained consistent.

Another consistent trend among community college faculty is the
increase in the average number of credit hours taught. In 1988, part-time faculty reported teaching an average of 7.5 credit hours each week; that figure
increased to 8.5 hours per week in the 2004 survey. Similarly, full-timers taught
an average of 15.5 hours per week in 1988 compared to 17.8 hours in 2004.

Although the number of credit hours taught by full- and part-time faculty
has risen over the years, salaries have not kept pace with the increased workload. The figures reported in Table 1.2 are in 2004 dollars so that comparisons
can be made across time. Although the average salary from the specific institution reported by part-time faculty increased substantially between 1988 and
1993, that average dropped in 1999 and 2004. The data from full-time faculty
demonstrate a slightly different trend: average salaries from the institution
increased modestly between 1988 and 1993, dropped slightly in 1999, and
then rose again in 2004. The trends in total income reported by part- and full-
time faculty are similar to the salary trends. Part-timers saw a significant
increase in total income between 1988 and 1993 and then a steady drop in
1999 and 2004. The average total income reported by full-timers increased
between 1988 and 1993, dropped in 1999, and increased again in 2004.

In addition to significant differences in salaries, part-time and full-time
faculty have substantial differences in their average length of employment
at their home institution. Full-time faculty saw an increase in their average
employment duration from 11.3 years in 1993 to 12.2 years in 2004. Similarly, part-timers' average employment period at a single institution increased
from 5.9 years in 1993 to 7.0 years in 2004. Although part-time faculty have
been employed at their respective institution for considerably shorter times
than full-time faculty, their average length of employment provides evidence
that contradicts the popular stereotype of transience and instability.

NEW DIRECTIONS FOR COMMUNITY COLLEGES • DOI: 10.1002/cc

Table 1.2. Employment Characteristics of Full- and Part-Time Faculty

	Part-Time Faculty				Full-Time Faculty			
	1988	1993	1999	2004	1988	1993	1999	2004
Principal activity								
Teaching		93.0	93.6	92.5		83.3	84.0	82.5
Research		0.4	0.0	0.0		0.3	0.3	0.1
Administration		1.2	1.5	0.6		10.4	9.5	8.6
Other		5.4	4.9	6.9		6.0	6.2	8.8
Field								
Arts and humanities	21.6	25.6	27.4	23.9	19.4	22.1	22.4	20.9
Science and engineering	33.4	31.8	33.3	33.2	34.6	35.4	35.4	37.7
Social sciences and education	11.1	14.0	16.1	16.9	17.1	16.2	13.0	16.5
Business	17.4	9.8	7.3	6.5	11.0	9.4	9.6	7.0
Other fields	16.6	18.9	15.9	19.6	17.9	16.9	19.7	17.9
Average class hours	7.5	7.6	8.4	8.5	15.5	16.1	17.1	17.8
Finances								
Basic salary (2004)	$7,500	$13,370	$11,097	$8,990	$51,450	$52,390	$50,630	$52,600
Total income (2004)	$44,260	$55,630	$45,650	$43,850	$61,300	$64,050	$60,970	$63,620
Average years at current institution		5.9	6.3	7.0		11.3	12.2	12.2
Academic appointment at another institution				10.7				2.8
Other employment outside this institution	78.4	78.5	54.1	71.8	27.3	26.7	20.7	16.2

Data from the 2004 NSOPF provide further evidence to refute the assumption that the majority of part-time community college faculty have instructional appointments at more than one postsecondary institution. Less than 11 percent of part-time community college faculty reported having a faculty appointment, either full or part time, at another postsecondary institution. This finding supports prior research concluding that a small percentage of part-time faculty have teaching appointments at more than one institution (Gappa and Leslie, 1997; Leslie and Gappa, 2002). In contrast, nearly 72 percent of part-time faculty indicated having at least one job outside their part-time position. Many of these part-timers hold full-time employment in other professional fields. Approximately 16 percent of full-time faculty report having more than one job; however, many of these full-time faculty members report serving as consultants for other institutions, nonprofit organizations, or businesses.

Finally, the percentage time spent by both part-time and full-time faculty on professional development activities has increased over the years. In 1988, part-time faculty reported spending 3.5 percent of their time on professional development; that figure rose to 5.9 percent in 1999. Similarly, full-time faculty indicated that 2.4 percent of their time in 1988 was spent on professional development compared to 6.5 percent of their time in 1999.

Employment Satisfaction and Beliefs

Many believe that part-time community college faculty are dissatisfied with their appointment (Mangan, 1991). Trends in the NSOPF data, however, suggest just the opposite: part-timers are becoming more satisfied with the terms of their employment. Overall, job satisfaction among part-time and full-time faculty was essentially the same across all of the NSOPF administrations. In 1988, roughly 90 percent of full- and part-time faculty indicated they were somewhat or very satisfied with their job, and that figure increased slightly to 92 percent in 2004 for both faculty types.

Although part-timers indicate an overwhelming sense of satisfaction with their jobs, some frustration exists. Part-time faculty report being most dissatisfied with the benefits provided through their community college appointment. However, this dissatisfaction has diminished over the years, as 70 percent of part-time faculty reported being dissatisfied with benefits in 1988, while in 2004, only 49.4 indicated they were very dissatisfied or somewhat dissatisfied with their benefit packages. In comparison, 19.1 percent of full-time faculty indicated a level of dissatisfaction with benefits in 1988 versus 13.2 percent in 2004.

In a similar trend, the proportion of part-time faculty dissatisfied with their salaries from their respective institutions decreased between 1988 and 2004; 37.5 percent of part-timers were dissatisfied with salaries in 1988 versus 29.9 percent in 2004. This figure is somewhat surprising given the previously reported salary trends. Part-timers have become more satisfied with their salaries even though they have remained fairly constant over the sixteen-year span of the surveys. Interestingly, full-time faculty appear to be just as dissatisfied with their salaries as part-time faculty: 33.3 percent of full-timers reported being dissatisfied in 1988 versus 27.3 percent in 2004.

Satisfaction with job security demonstrates an expected trend, as 85 percent of full-time faculty report being satisfied with job security between 1988 and 1999, while just 56.8 percent of part-timers indicate feeling somewhat or very secure in their jobs. The short-term contracts offered to part-time faculty contribute significantly to their feelings of insecurity (Rhoades, 1996).

Part-time faculty appear to be much more satisfied with their workload compared to their full-time colleagues. Nearly 90 percent of part-time faculty reported being somewhat or very satisfied with their workload in the 2004 NSOPF. In contrast, 76 percent of full-timers responded in the same way. Although the short-term contracts offered to part-time faculty may contribute to a greater sense of job insecurity, part-timer faculty generally have the ability to set the parameters of their workload. In contrast, full-time faculty may be asked to teach an extra course during a term or assume additional administrative responsibilities.

In regard to autonomy as instructors, part- and full-time faculty report being equally satisfied in their abilities to decide the content of the courses they teach, as 95 percent of both part- and full-time faculty reported being somewhat or very satisfied with this aspect of their position in 2004. Part-timers indicate they are less satisfied than their full-time counterparts in their ability to decide the courses they teach. Between 1988 and 1999, less than 75 percent of part-time faculty reported feeling satisfied with the authority granted to them to decide the courses they teach, while more than 85 percent of full-timers felt very or somewhat satisfied.

A significantly smaller proportion of full-time faculty, compared to part-timers, reported feeling satisfied with the academic quality of undergraduates in their courses. In 1999, slightly more than two-thirds of full-time faculty felt satisfied with the quality of undergraduates, and three-fourths of part-timers responded similarly.

On survey items in 2004 that related to fair treatment and recognition in the workplace, part-time faculty tended to take a more positive view than their full-time colleagues. Nearly 83 percent of part-time faculty agreed that teaching was rewarded at their respective institution, while just more than 76 percent of full-timers felt the same way. Interestingly, a higher percentage of part-time faculty agreed that part-timers were treated fairly at their institution. More than 75 percent of part-time faculty somewhat or strongly agreed that part-time faculty were treated fairly, while just over 65 percent of full-timers agreed.

Pedagogical Practices

The NSOPF administrations asked a variety of questions about the teaching methods faculty used in the classroom; however, these questions were not consistent across the four survey administrations. Part-time and full-time faculty were equally as likely to use essay (45 percent versus 48 percent) and short-answer (54 percent versus 59 percent) questions on midterms and finals. Full-time faculty more frequently reported having their students write multiple drafts of papers, and they were more likely to assign term papers to their students than their part-time colleagues did. The most substantial difference in pedagogies of part-time and full-time faculty was in assigning group projects: more than 60 percent of full-timers required students to work in groups in at least some of their classes, while just more than 45 percent of part-timers had the same requirement.

These statistics for classroom pedagogy merely describe differences between part-time and full-time faculty. Because the data do not allow specific controls for the types of courses taught by part-timers and full-timers, it is difficult to draw conclusions about differences in pedagogical quality. Part-time faculty may assign group projects and term papers less frequently because the content or field of their courses does not lend itself to such assignments.

In addition to classroom pedagogy, the 2004 NSOPF included questions about technology use. In at least one area, full-time faculty far outpaced their part-time colleagues in using technology. Nearly 50 percent of full-time faculty reported having class Web sites, while less than 25 percent of part-timers used Web sites for their courses. Although this difference in Web site use is substantial, full-time faculty likely have greater access to institutional support staff, such as technology professionals, who assist them in maintaining these Web sites.

Conclusion

This descriptive analysis has demonstrated a number of similarities among part- and full-time faculty. Demographic characteristics of part-timers and full-timers are remarkably similar. As expected, the most substantial difference emerged in the level of education achieved by the two faculty types. The educational disparities between part- and full-time faculty likely represent differences in career priorities, as full-timers have sought a career in academia, while many part-timer faculty have full-time careers in other fields that may require less education.

Among the various employment characteristics measured by the NSOPF, part-time faculty more closely resemble their full-time counterparts, which provides evidence to the contrary of popular assumptions about part-time faculty. The data suggest that part-time faculty maintain stable employment with their institutions, as their length of employment at their respective institution averaged seven years in 2004. Similarly, part-time faculty's overall job satisfaction parallels that of full-time faculty. Indeed, part-time faculty are even more satisfied than their full-time counterparts in their average workload. Although there is a common assumption that part-time faculty members are dissatisfied and highly transient individuals (Haeger, 1998), analyses of the NSOPF data suggest otherwise.

Umbach (2007) suggested that part-time faculty are significantly more disengaged than their full-time colleagues, and Haeger (1998) indicated that part-time faculty threaten the quality of academic programs; however, the pedagogical practices of part-time faculty do not necessarily support these arguments. Part-time faculty use the same teaching practices about as frequently as full-timers, and any differences in pedagogy may be attributed to differences in course content or discipline. Although NSOPF data suggest that part-time faculty share similar teaching practices with their full-time counterparts, the surveys do not adequately measure the integration of part-time faculty into the departmental or campus culture. Lack of offices, support staff, and inclusion in departmental and campus meetings may prevent part-time faculty from becoming fully integrated into the life of the institution (Haeger, 1998). Future research needs to address factors that affect any differences in teaching methods and campus integration between part-time and full-time faculty.

Part-time faculty represent a diverse group of individuals. Future research needs to disaggregate this complex group to analyze potential differences within it. As the use of part-time faculty continues to grow in community colleges and in four-year institutions, administrators and policymakers need to continue to develop their understanding of the needs and characteristics of this component of the academic labor force.

References

Cataldi, E. F., Fahimi, M., Bradburn, E. M., and Zimbler, L. *2004 National Study of Post-Secondary Faculty Report on Faculty and Instructional Staff.* Washington, D.C.: U.S. Department of Education, 2005.

Cohen, A. M., and Brawer, F. B. *The American Community College.* (4th ed.) San Francisco: Jossey-Bass, 2003.

Gappa, J. M., and Leslie, D. W. *Two Faculties or One? The Conundrum of Part-Timers in a Bifurcated Work Force.* Washington, D.C.: American Association for Higher Education, 1997.

Grubb, N. W. *Honored But Invisible: An Inside Look at Teaching in Community Colleges.* New York: Routledge, 1999.

Haeger, J. D. "Part-Time Faculty, Quality Programs, and Economic Realities." In D. W. Leslie (ed.), *The Growing Use of Part-time Faculty: Understanding Causes and Effects.* San Francisco: Jossey-Bass, 1998.

Heuer, R., and others. *2004 National Study of Postsecondary Faculty Methodology Report.* Washington, D.C.: U.S. Department of Education, 2006.

Leslie, D. W., and Gappa, J. M. "Part-Time Faculty: Competent and Committed." In C. L. Outcalt (ed.), *Community College Faculty: Characteristics, Practices, and Challenges.* New Directions for Community College, no. 118. San Francisco: Jossey-Bass, 2002.

Mangan, K. "Many Colleges Will Fill Vacancies with Part-Time Professors, Citing Economy and Uncertainty About Enrollments." *Chronicle of Higher Education,* Aug. 7, 1991, pp. A9–A10.

Rhoades G. "Reorganizing the Faculty Workforce for Flexibility: Part-Time Professional Labor." *Journal of Higher Education,* 1996, *67*(6), 626–659.

Umbach, P.D. "How Effective Are They? Exploring the Impact of Contingent Faculty on Undergraduate Education." *Review of Higher Education,* 2007, *30*(2), 91–123.

KEVIN EAGAN is a doctoral student in higher education at the University of California, Los Angeles.

NEW DIRECTIONS FOR COMMUNITY COLLEGES • DOI: 10.1002/cc

2

Part-time faculty are best understood as extensions of institutional identity. In the twenty-first century, the identity of community colleges makes part-time faculty central to the organization's goals.

Multiple Judgments: Institutional Context and Part-Time Faculty

John S. Levin

Part-time faculty members at community colleges are customarily understood from an institutional perspective that is based on traditional conceptions of the community college as a component of a tiered educational system (high school, community college, four-year college or university). This conception places the community college in the role of either a junior college or a training school. This traditional conception highlights academic preparation, skills development, and sequential learning and justifies the institution's worth through proxies such as degree attainment, job placement, and percentage of students who transfer to a four-year college or university. It is this conception that has been used to examine the role and condition of part-time faculty, conflating those at community colleges with those at universities and aggregating all part-time faculty as if they were part of this traditional conception. From this perspective, part-time faculty are viewed as either marginal or deleterious to the community college mission of student advancement.

Yet there are other ways of viewing and understanding the community college distinct from the traditional conception. For example, I have used the term *new world college* to describe the behaviors and actions of community colleges that place them in a globalized and competitive economy (Levin, 2007). These institutions are components of the new liberalized world of economic global competition and are decidedly distinct from their old world, or European-generated, conceptions of higher education institutions, particularly universities—even those found in former European

WILEY
InterScience®
DISCOVER SOMETHING GREAT

NEW DIRECTIONS FOR COMMUNITY COLLEGES, no. 140, Winter 2007 © 2007 Wiley Periodicals, Inc.
Published online in Wiley InterScience (www.interscience.wiley.com) • DOI: 10.1002/cc.300

colonies such as the United States, Canada, and Australia. In such a new world, community colleges have decidedly multiple functions and institutional identities that align them with adroit businesses, in a condition that Gee, Hull, and Lankshear (1996) and others call "fast capitalism." With multiple purposes that go beyond schooling, community colleges combine characteristics of social services agencies, training arms of business and industry, adult education centers, rehabilitation centers (think of prison education), and community developers. Furthermore, the expansion of mission that has led to the community college baccalaureate degree and the postbaccalaureate degree reshapes the junior college and training school beyond recognition. Colleges now have educational services for the severely mentally and physically impaired and partnerships with universities to offer master's degrees on campus. The range is broad indeed.

By framing the community college as a business or as an agent of economic development, we need to rethink our view of faculty work and faculty status to the extent that part-time faculty are central, not peripheral, to the community college enterprise. This centrality is based on the rationale of the efficiency and effectiveness of institutional operations. Part-time faculty are an economic necessity and provide institutional adaptation to changing circumstances. Moreover, some part-time faculty are more central and valuable than others, which indicates that viewing all part-time faculty in the same manner is misleading (Levin, Kater, and Wagoner, 2006).

Part-time faculty members in the community college are products of the conception of the institution: their condition as a labor force is identified by institutional context. The context for community colleges is largely one that is economic in its orientation and functioning. In order to fit the more ethically compelling mission of educational access into this context, community college practitioners must perform magic tricks: they must convince both the public and the private sectors that community colleges are critical to the state or region's economic prosperity, and they must endeavor to rescue students from a dissatisfying present or ill-fated future. They offer hope and promise to the disadvantaged of our society and at the same time justify their outcomes as economically productive. The argument that helps in this rationale is made to state legislators by community college presidents, such as one president from a Pacific Northwest community college: "Why are we spending so much money on incarcerating people and so little money on educating them? And that goes from pre-kindergarten all the way through with community colleges being a big part of that. So let's quit spending all of this money on juvenile justice and incarcerating and making new rules to incarcerate people."

The community college as new world college, then, is subject to what one former community college president claimed to his college constituents, in a letter I collected for an earlier publication: "All of us are aware, the tides of change are sweeping across our country, not only in a political sense but to the very core of our business, industrial, financial, governmental and educational enterprises. In this highly competitive global economy, change is no longer an intellectual activity to analyze and discuss, it has in every sense become a mechanism of survival—a way of life—regardless of where one looks. Re-structuring, re-engineering, re-framing, downsizing, whatever you call it—it is with us and we must deal with it" (Levin, 2001, p. 67).

In a knowledge-based economy, information technologies become not only the conveyors of communication but also the tools and mechanisms that structure work. This includes teaching, which in the community college is the core activity of the organization. Teaching is redefined as information processing and disseminating, and those who teach have seen their work altered. One example is seen in work hours and student access to faculty as noted by a science faculty member at a California community college, whose work week adds up to about fifty-six hours: "I'd say I work forty hours per week—that's not teaching time—but I work from home. I have a home office. A lot of students e-mail me at home, and I respond to them from home. I tell them if they send me an e-mail, I'll respond quickly. So, I'm available through the weekend. I check my e-mail regularly through the weekend. . . . I'm consistently on-call since I make myself available via e-mail." At that same college, the faculty senate president articulates the pace of change and the increase in work for faculty: "We are always moving, never reflecting on projects, always go, go, go. . . . There are a lot of pluses and minuses to this kind of system—a lot of pressure. . . . With more computers, the faculty workload went way up." A faculty member who is a union official at a Pacific Northwest college also discussed the organizational changes that affect faculty work: "Overall campus restructuring has brought about a downsizing of support staff. Now that most [faculty] have computers, they are expected to do the secretarial and administrative things themselves."

Furthermore, the change in student demographics over the past two decades has challenged faculty approaches to instruction. One faculty member who teaches in the general educational development testing program at a Chicago community college reflects on his students and their characteristics:

> I have some immigrants [who] for various reasons either didn't graduate from high school or their records are destroyed or they can't get them, because they are refugees or whatever. Typical age has become younger and younger. It use to be, back in the 80s when I was teaching this class, my average age would to be thirty-five or forty. Now, my average age is twenty-five or twenty-eight. People drop out of high school, or they never finish. They drop out for a million different reasons. Usually it has to do with kids that are poor; their friends are into drugs; they want to go out and play; there is alcoholism or drug problems in the family; they have to go to work; they are pregnant: you know, all of those kind of things, plus a million different other stories.

Indeed, in the twenty-first century, the community college student body is a diverse one, which presents considerable frustrations and dilemmas for faculty, as noted by a basic skills instructor in North Carolina:

> Our students are as diverse as the phone book. . . . There are times when as an instructor and as a human being I want to do everything on earth for them. There are other times when I would like to strangle them and make them completely disappear. Most of them have had challenges all of their life. Most of them have no encouragement at home. A lot . . . have been told all their lives that they're nobody and nothing and they will never amount to anything. So they've been put down. I try to be honest with my students. I tell them exactly like it is. They appreciate that. If they have done well, I tell them that, but I don't sugar coat it. . . . I don't make them think that they've. . . gone beyond the limits. . . . Sometimes we always like to think about the good ones. I worry about the ones that fall between the cracks. I always worry about the ones that drop out. They come for a while and then they drop out, and we never hear from them again. I often wonder what happens to them. Sometimes they come back. And then sometimes they never do . . . and you wonder what, if you did something wrong or just what happened in that process.

The considerable range of students makes traditional approaches to instruction problematical and makes a myth of the customary concept of a postsecondary faculty member who is a full-time employee, teaches a group of young students who recently graduated from high school, uses a traditional teaching format, gives weekly assignments, and holds office hours for student meetings on their work.

Faculty Differences by Program Area

There is both evidence and scholarship to indicate that there are not only demographic differences among part-time faculty by program area but also by employment satisfaction level (U.S. Department of Education, 2003; Levin, Kater, and Wagoner, 2006; Wagoner, 2004). Current research suggests that humanities and social sciences part-time faculty members are less satisfied with their condition as part-time faculty than those in occupational and vocational areas. While compensation is one plausible explanation for differences in satisfaction (Levin, Kater, and Wagoner, 2006), another explanation is that the organizational context and the institution's orientation to a globally competitive economy are more compatible with part-time faculty in particular program areas. A new world college is conducive to a faculty that is not only part time but also aligned in their expertise and instructional responsibilities with the demands of the economic marketplace.

Liberal arts faculty are essentially hired not for their expertise but rather for their labor as substitutes for full-time faculty. Part-time faculty in this area are less expensive than full-time faculty; they can and do teach large numbers of students, many of whom will not advance to higher levels or find their way to the labor market in their academic areas. The economic benefits of this stratum of faculty allow community colleges to fulfill their access role: inexpensive labor for student enrollments.

NEW DIRECTIONS FOR COMMUNITY COLLEGES • DOI: 10.1002/cc

In general, occupational and professional program faculty are hired for their specialized knowledge or because of labor market shortages of full-time faculty. While these part-time faculty members are less expensive than full-time faculty and thus an economic benefit to the institution, they have expertise that the institution needs and is not readily available. Unlike the majority of liberal arts faculty, they do not have full-time employment aspirations at a community college.

We can assert that there are two distinct strata of part-time faculty: those who are contract labor and those who are specialized labor. Both groups reflect a developing condition of the community college. On the one hand, the community college mission of access and state financing based on enrollments presses the institution to the limits of performance by adding more and more students. On the other hand, the community college, as a vehicle of economic development and labor market provider of a trained workforce, emulates the practices of business and industry and endeavors to satisfy their expectations for what are termed employability skills (Levin, 2001). These include employees who are designed to fit employer requirements. Who knows better about these requirements than those who work in business and industry? Thus, part-time faculty in such areas as nursing, business, and technology and in newly established postbaccalaureate teaching certificate programs are corporate trainers for their fields, not traditional faculty as understood in the literature on community college faculty (Grubb, 1999; McGrath and Spear, 1991; Richardson, Fisk, and Okun, 1983; Seidman, 1985).

Both strata are central to the community college and indeed characterize the community college as an institution that revolves around two goals: the goal of efficiency and the goal of workforce development. *Goals* here refers to actions, not simply intentions, of the organization (Mintzberg, 1983). This is not to say that effective education and training are not part of the community college's purposes, but these are enacted as strategies that will support the legitimacy of the institution and satisfy its constituents. The multieducational purposes of the community college codified in state legislation—provider of university preparation or parallel education, vocational and occupational education, community and continuing education, and basic skills or remediation—are not the sole and permanent claim of the institution if it does not meet its two prime goals of efficiency and workforce development. In these goals, part-time faculty are the critical components of the community college.

Implications

This rather austere view of the community college justifies the continuation of the high level—67 percent of all faculty—of employment of part-time faculty. As long as community colleges continue to develop along the lines of an institution characterized as a new world college, part-time faculty will occupy a critical place. While some argue that the practice of high levels of part-time employment is unethical, unfair labor practice, irresponsible, exploitative, and the like (Gappa and Leslie, 1997; Rhoades, 1998; Roueche, Roueche, and Milliron, 1995; Wagoner, Metcalfe, and Olaore, 2005), they refrain from challenging the goals of the institution—goals that are the basis of the practice. In order to change the practice, community college goals must be altered.

References

Gappa, J. M., and Leslie, D. W. *Two Faculties or One? The Conundrum of Part-Timers in a Bifurcated Work Force.* Washington, D.C.: American Association for Higher Education, 1997

Gee, J. P., Hull, G., and Lankshear, C. *The New Work Order: Behind the Language of the New Capitalism.* Boulder, Colo.: Westview Press, 1996.

Grubb, N. W. *Honored But Invisible: An Inside Look at Teaching in Community Colleges.* New York: Routledge, 1999.

Levin, J. *Globalizing the Community College: Strategies for Change in the Twenty-First Century.* New York: Palgrave, 2001.

Levin, J. "Neo-Liberal Policies and Community College Faculty Work." In J. Smart and W. Tierney (eds.), *Handbook of Higher Education.* Norwell, Mass.: Kluwer, 2007.

Levin, J., Kater, S., and Wagoner, R. *Community College Faculty: At Work in the New Economy.* New York: Palgrave, 2006.

McGrath, D., and Spear, M. *The Academic Crisis of the Community College.* Albany: State University of New York Press, 1991.

Mintzberg, H. *Power in and Around Organizations.* Upper Saddle River, N.J.: Prentice Hall, 1983.

Rhoades, G. *Managed Professionals: Unionized Faculty and Restructuring Academic Labor.* Albany: State University of New York Press, 1998.

Richardson, R., Fisk, E., and Okun, M. *Literacy in the Open-Access College.* San Francisco: Jossey-Bass, 1983.

Roueche, J., Roueche, S., and Milliron, M. *Strangers in Their Own Land: Part-Time Faculty in American Community Colleges.* Washington, D.C.: Community College Press, 1995.

Seidman, E. *In the Words of the Faculty.* San Francisco: Jossey-Bass, 1985.

Wagoner, R. "The Contradictory Faculty: Part-Time Faculty at Community Colleges." Unpublished doctoral dissertation, University of Arizona, 2004.

Wagoner, R. L., Metcalfe, A. S., and Olaore, I. "Fiscal Reality and Academic Quality: Part-Time Faculty and the Challenge to Organizational Culture at Community Colleges." *Community College Journal of Research and Practice,* 2005, 29, 1–20.

U.S. Department of Education. *National Study of Postsecondary Faculty.* Washington, D.C.: U.S. Department of Education, 2003.

JOHN S. LEVIN is the Bank of America Professor of Education Leadership and director of the California Community College Collaborative at the University of California, Riverside.

3

This chapter analyzes data from the 1999 National Study of Postsecondary Faculty to suggest that community college part-time faculty can be understood as temporary labor in the new economy.

Globalization, the New Economy, and Part-Time Faculty

Richard L. Wagoner

As John Levin noted in Chapter Two, how part-time faculty are viewed depends on the organizational mission of the particular community college. In this chapter, I present an argument for how part-time faculty at community colleges can be conceptualized and understood as new economy labor. Initially I review the literature regarding part-time, temporary labor in the new economy and then develop a specific characterization of how this might be understood in terms of part-time faculty at community colleges. Finally, I present an analysis of data from the 1999 National Study of Postsecondary Faculty (NSOPF 99) to demonstrate how community college part-time faculty resemble this conceptualization in terms of their incomes, employment patterns, and perceptions of their positions at colleges.

New Economy Labor

Perhaps the most striking effect of the new economy on labor is that it has isolated individual workers while allowing institutions to increase efficiency and flexibility (see Chapter Seven). Castells (2000) argues that the most fundamental transformation in work and employment is "the individualization of work and the fragmentation of societies" (p. 217). Individuals must fend for themselves in the marketplace, with no protections from the government or unions (Osterman, Kochan, Locke, and Piore, 2001). Ultimately, then, there is the potential for a fortunate few individuals to reap considerable rewards, but many others will be exploited (Carnoy, 2000). Smith

(2001) equates the differences in potential rewards to a great divide; in order to cross this divide, workers must be willing to take increased individual risks. This idea is in direct contrast to the social contract that governed employee and employer relations throughout the mid- and late twentieth century (Osterman, Kochan, Locke, and Piore, 2001).

This form of individualization and the divide it creates has resulted in two distinct types of part-time labor in the new economy. Those temporary laborers, who are most likely to be recruited and valued by the companies and institutions that hire them, possess skills and expertise that are important to institutions across different sectors. The more an individual's skills are valuable to multiple organizations across several sectors, the more that individual will be valued and the more that individual will desire to sell her or his skills to multiple buyers in an open labor market (Castells, 2000; Carnoy, 2000). Clearly the new economy offers a heady proposition to anyone who possesses skills valued in multiple business sectors. On the other side of the gulf of temporary labor are those who do not possess rare, highly valued skills and abilities. These part-timers do not have numerous opportunities in multiple industries. This lack of employment options causes these part-timers to seek full-time, stable employment with the institution where they are employed (Smith, 2001). Their predicament is exacerbated because a surplus of individuals can perform their duties as competently as they are able. Companies and institutions, in an effort to embody the values of efficiency and flexibility central to globalization and the new economy, are reluctant to promote these part-timers to full-time status (Smith, 2001). Because organizations depend on each type of temporary worker described, the categories are not mutually exclusive. Both types of part-timers can be found in the same institution simultaneously.

Part-time faculty at community colleges have also been described in similar terms. Jacobs (1998) points out that the use of part-time faculty increases the prestige and effectiveness of institutions because part-timers bring skills, abilities, and talents not found in a college's permanent, full-time faculty. These individuals are distinguished by their impressive experience as well as their highly valued skills. Generally the majority of these individuals have either full-time employment outside the college or are retired.

While acknowledging this traditional use of adjunct labor, other scholars have suggested that the rising problem of part-time faculty in higher education does not center on this use, but rather on their use as a convenient and expedient means to lower costs and increase flexibility for institutions (Gappa and Leslie, 1993; Rhoades, 1998; Roueche, Roueche, and Milliron, 1995; Wyles, 1998; Benjamin, 2002). This practice has increased dramatically as the percentage of part-time faculty has grown over the past thirty years. These part-time faculty members are frequently viewed as less skilled and trained than full-time faculty; the quality of their instruction and their dedication to the institution are questioned as well.

NEW DIRECTIONS FOR COMMUNITY COLLEGES • DOI: 10.1002/cc

These two views of the use of part-time faculty reveal an important contradiction: part-time faculty as highly skilled and trained assets and part-time faculty as a less-skilled means to achieve efficiency, flexibility, and control. This contradiction is tied to the transfer and vocational functions of community colleges. Those individuals who are not academics but have an educational background in academic disciplines do not necessarily possess skills and training beyond those of full-time faculty in community colleges. However, those with advanced training and experience in specific vocational areas who are not full-time faculty are likely to possess skills that full-time vocational faculty do not. That is, it is reasonable to assume that on average, a higher percentage of part-time faculty from vocational fields bring rare and valued skills to community colleges than part-time faculty from academic fields. From this perspective, vocational faculty who are part time fit the highly valued, traditional definition of part-timer, while transfer faculty who are part time fit the definition of part-timers as a means to efficiency, flexibility, and control.

Clearly this perspective has led to a contradictory labor market where temporary employees work side by side with permanent employees. Although both groups serve similar functions, part-time employees have little choice than to negotiate this potentially exploitative market on their own; those with rare skills and abilities may be valued commodities in numerous markets, while those with common skills find themselves on the wrong side of a labor market chasm. The lens of new economy labor illuminates at least two bifurcations in community college faculty: one between full-time and part-time faculty and one among various types of part-timers.

Finally, a conceptualization of community college part-time faculty emerges from this perspective. Resembling the strata of temporary labor in the new economy who possess rare and highly valued skills, the first type of part-time faculty at community colleges are faculty members with strong employment options outside academe. These close ties to the private sector create a distinct profile. These faculty members are less dependent on their income from colleges because of well-paying employment outside academe. As a result, they do not perceive themselves as exploited financially. Professional careers and contacts outside academe also contribute to less alienation and higher levels of satisfaction for these faculty members because they do not require their college employment to fulfill their need for an active professional life. Given this general profile, it follows that analysis of national data will reveal that these part-timers earn a majority of their income from nonacademic sources, earn more income from all sources than other part-timers, and tend to be employed full time in a position outside academe (Levin, Kater, and Wagoner, 2006).

A mirror image of the group above, the second stratum of community college part-time faculty resembles the type of new economy temporary labor that does not possess rare and highly valued skills, causing them to be employed as a means for the institution to achieve increased managerial control through economic efficiency and labor force flexibility. Therefore, analysis of national data should indicate that these part-time faculty are dependent primarily on academic careers for both their livelihoods and their professional identities, leading them to be dependent on income from academic employment and to work part time at other academic institutions in an effort to create an academic career (Levin, Kater, and Wagoner, 2006).

Analysis of NSOPF 99 Data

Using the faculty conceptualization presented in this chapter and modeling both the seven-group faculty disaggregation described by Levin, Kater, and Wagoner (2006) and Benjamin's division (1998) between the liberal arts cluster and the vocationally oriented cluster of community college faculty, I created a two-group disaggregation for community college faculty for analyzing the NSOPF 99 data. Although this disaggregation does not offer as nuanced an analysis as the seven-group disaggregation, it expands the number of academic fields Benjamin (1998) included in his earlier analysis. The two groups are the traditional arts and sciences (arts and humanities, social and behavioral sciences, and physical and biological sciences) and vocational and technical training (computing and technology, professions, and trades and services). NSOPF 99 presented responses from 4,560 faculty at 269 community colleges. To ensure consistency in the data, faculty members who provided valid responses to all questions discussed here are in the analysis, resulting in a total of 4,283 faculty members—1,572 full time and 2,711 part time. The traditional arts and sciences group contains 755 full-time faculty members and 1,458 part-time faculty, and the vocational and technical training group contains 583 full-timers and 892 part-timers. Because some fields do not fit precisely with either of the two groups, they are omitted from either group but are included in the all-faculty categories.

Faculty members who comprise the traditional arts and sciences are assumed to resemble the type of new economy temporary labor that possesses training and abilities that are neither rare nor highly valued, resulting in few employment options and relatively low pay. Put another way, this stratum of new economy labor is exploited in the pursuit of efficiency and flexibility. Conversely, faculty members who comprise the vocational and technical group are assumed to resemble the upper stratum of new economy temporary labor because of their employment options outside academe, their more valued skills and training within colleges, and their relatively high income. I will discuss results from the analysis based on the hypotheses that rise from the faculty conceptualization presented earlier: faculty income, including total income and sources of income; faculty perceptions of their community college position; their desire for a full-time academic position; and the status and sector of their outside employment.

The data for mean total earned income demonstrate important results in themselves. On average, part-time faculty earned an income from all sources of $40,226, and full-time college faculty earned a total of $53,989.

While the overall aggregate incomes for part- and full-time faculty are significantly different, they appear to be reasonably close to one another, a point supported by Gappa and Leslie (1997). But when community college faculty are disaggregated, a different picture begins to emerge. With a total income of $37,556, part-timers from the arts and sciences group earn less than the average of all part-timers and earn proportionally less when compared to full-time faculty in their group (31 percent less). Conversely, part-time faculty from the vocational and training group average more income ($47,144) than all part-timers and earn a higher proportion of income when compared to full-time faculty (85 percent). Already it is clear that there are significant income differences that aggregate data hide. Those differences are amplified when the sources of total income are analyzed separately.

The total income category looks at three separate sources of income: institutional income, income from other higher education institutions, and nonacademic income. All full-time faculty, regardless of academic discipline, earn over 80 percent of their income from their home institution. However, the results for part-time faculty vary considerably. Part-timers from the arts and sciences earn more than half (55 percent) of their income from academic sources, while those from the vocational and training group earn less than one-third (30 percent) of their income from the same sources. While it is true that arts and sciences part-time faculty depend on nonacademic income to survive, they attempt to earn as much as possible from academic sources. It is also important to note that vocational and training part-time faculty members earn almost as much from nonacademic sources ($33,120) as the arts and sciences group earns from all sources.

Taken together, these three income variables clearly illuminate the differences in total earned income. Members of the vocational and training group earn significantly more income than members of the arts and sciences group. The source of the majority of the income earned by the vocational group is work conducted outside an academic setting, while members of the arts and sciences group earn much more of their total income from academic sources, with an important reliance on nonacademic income to survive. Simply put, the arts and sciences group relies on academic employment for their livelihoods, while members of the vocational and training group supplement their incomes with academic work.

The differences demonstrated by the results for income data are also reflected in part-time faculty members' responses to questions about how they perceive their positions at community colleges and in their desire for full-time employment at those colleges. When asked if they view the study institution as their primary employer, members of the arts and sciences group were 80 percent (15 percentage points) more likely to respond that they did view the study institution as their primary employment when compared to part-timers from the vocational and training group. Similar findings resulted from part-time faculty members' responses to why they were employed part time at the institution. Once again, part-timers from the arts and sciences group were two-thirds (12 percentage points) as likely to indicate that they desired full-time employment but none was available when compared to their counterparts from the vocational and training group. These results add credence to the assumption that part-time faculty from the traditional academic areas identify themselves primarily as academics, while part-time faculty from the vocation and training areas of community colleges gain their professional identity outside academe.

The source of the professional identity for part-time faculty in the training and vocational fields is evident in the results for their status of employment outside the study institution and the sector of that employment. Part-timers from the training and vocational fields were approximately two-thirds more likely to work in a full-time position outside their study institution than were part-time faculty from the arts and sciences. With respect to the sector in which part-time faculty work outside their community college, members of the vocational and training group were twice as likely to work in a nonacademic setting. Again, there is strong evidence to suggest that part-time faculty members from the training and vocational areas of community colleges gain their professional identity from nonacademic employment.

To summarize, the analysis has explored income data, part-time faculty perceptions of their employment, and the status and sector of any noninstitutional employment that part-timers hold. In each case, the results have supported the conceptualization of community college part-time faculty as a form of new economy temporary labor. The income data indicate a significant difference in the incomes of full- and part-time faculty, even in the aggregate. Furthermore, those differences are more acute for members of the arts and sciences group than they are for members of the vocational and training group. While all full-time faculty earn the overwhelming majority of their income from the study institution, the results are different for part-time faculty. Members of the vocational and training group tend to earn much more of their income in nonacademic jobs and tend to hold full-time positions in addition to this employment. Part-time members of the arts and sciences group, who earn significantly less than the vocational group, tend to earn the majority of their income from postsecondary employment and also tend to have part-time status in these positions. There would seem to be, then, a substantial divide among part-time faculty regarding how, where, and to what level they earn a living—a divide resembling the one scholars have suggested exists in the new economy.

Conclusion

While the data analysis in this chapter suggests that part-time faculty do resemble the two aspects of new economy temporary labor found in the literature, one might be tempted to ask, So what? In the end, I believe the analysis in this chapter should indicate to community college practitioners and scholars alike that a one-size-fits-all conceptualization of part-time faculty perhaps fits no one's needs. Over the past ten to fifteen years, many colleges have made significant progress in their efforts to integrate part-timers into their campuses through support services that are identical for all part-timers, but the results of this chapter suggest that specialized policies for particular part-time groups might meet the needs of each group better than programs that conceptualize part-time faculty as an aggregate mass.

References

Benjamin, E. "Variations in the Characteristics of Part-Time Faculty by General Fields of Instruction and Research." In D. W. Leslie (ed.), *The Growing Use of Part-Time Faculty: Understanding Causes and Effects.* New Directions for Higher Education, no. 104. San Francisco: Jossey-Bass, 1998.

Benjamin, E. "How Over-Reliance on Contingent Appointments Diminishes Faculty Involvement in Student Learning." *Peer Review,* 2002, 5(1), 4–10.

Carnoy, M. *Sustaining the New Economy: Work, Family, and Community in the Information Age.* Cambridge, Mass.: Harvard University Press, 2000.

Castells, M. *The Rise of the Network Society.* (2nd ed.) Malden, Mass.: Blackwell, 2000.

Gappa, J. M., and Leslie, D. W. *The Invisible Faculty: Improving the Status of Part-Timers in Higher Education.* San Francisco: Jossey-Bass, 1993.

Gappa, J. M., and Leslie, D. W. *Two Faculties or One? The Conundrum of Part-Timers in a Bifurcated Work Force.* Washington, D.C.: American Association for Higher Education, 1997.

Jacobs, F. "Using Part-Time Faculty More Effectively." In D. W. Leslie (ed.), *The Growing Use of Part-Time Faculty: Understanding Causes and Effects.* New Directions for Higher Education, no. 104. San Francisco: Jossey-Bass, 1998.

Levin, J. S., Kater, S., and Wagoner, R. L. *Community College Faculty: At Work in the New Economy.* New York: Palgrave, 2006.

Osterman, P., Kochan, T. A., Locke, R. M., and Piore, M. J. *Working in America: A Blueprint for the New Labor Market.* Cambridge, Mass.: MIT Press, 2001.

Rhoades, G. *Managed Professionals: Unionized Faculty and Restructuring Academic Labor.* Albany: State University of New York Press, 1998.

Roueche, J. E., Roueche, S. D., and Milliron, M. D. *Strangers in Their Own Land: Part-Time Faculty in American Community Colleges.* Washington, D.C.: Community College Press, 1995.

Smith, V. *Crossing the Great Divide: Worker Risk and Opportunity in the New Economy.* Ithaca, N.Y.: Cornell University Press, 2001.

Wyles, B. A. "Adjunct Faculty in the Community College: Realities and Challenges." In D. W. Leslie (ed.), *The Growing Use of Part-Time Faculty: Understanding Causes and Effects.* New Directions for Higher Education, no. 104. San Francisco: Jossey-Bass, 1998.

RICHARD L. WAGONER *is assistant professor of higher education and organizational change in the Graduate School of Education and Information Studies at the University of California, Los Angeles.*

NEW DIRECTIONS FOR COMMUNITY COLLEGES • DOI: 10.1002/cc

4

This chapter addresses the use of adjunct faculty in community colleges. It examines issues of finding, hiring, orienting, evaluating, and developing adjuncts and stresses critical areas of ensuring quality and maintaining institutional standards.

Adjunct Faculty and the Continuing Quest for Quality

Donald W. Green

The role of part-time faculty in institutions of higher education has been a topic of discussion for many years. Currently there are half a million higher education adjunct faculty members in the United States. According to the U.S. Department of Education (2003), 66 percent of the faculty members teaching in community colleges are adjunct. This percentage varies by state, discipline, and type of program. For example, Rio Salado College in Tempe, Arizona, has only twenty-seven full-time faculty members but teaches 46,800 credit students and 14,000 noncredit students. Most of the classes are taught by the institution's one thousand adjunct faculty members (Maeroff, 2003). In general, community college adjunct faculty teach more than one course a semester, and 30 percent teach three or more classes per semester (Berger, Kirshstein, Zhang, and Carter, 2002). The more classes they teach, the more money the institution saves because of the pay differential with full-time faculty.

Given the cost savings, community colleges will continue to hire adjutant faculty. Moreover, these faculty members will continue to play a crucial role in fulfilling the institutional mission and will have an enormous impact on the institutional culture. At the same time, there are growing concerns about an institution's ratio of adjunct faculty to full-time faculty and its impact on the college. Therefore, it is critical for institutional leaders to explore the role that adjunct faculty play and to cultivate effective

DISCOVER SOMETHING GREAT

New Directions for Community Colleges, no. 140, Winter 2007 © 2007 Wiley Periodicals, Inc.
Published online in Wiley InterScience (www.interscience.wiley.com) • DOI: 10.1002/cc.302

professional development activities that will help them succeed in the community college environment.

To help part-time faculty, the college president or the academic vice president should develop a set of high expectations, have policies and practices in place, and provide ongoing development activities. Although each institution needs to tailor policies and practices to its needs, there are some standard practices that can make the task much easier. In this chapter, I discuss the rationale for hiring adjunct faculty, issues facing part-time faculty, quality in reference to teaching and professional development, and views of how to maintain high teaching standards and high student outcomes.

Why Use Adjunct Faculty?

A number of questions surround the use of adjunct faculty: Is there a standard ratio of full-time to part-time faculty that produces maximum effectiveness and efficiency? Are there differences in student learning outcomes between full-time and adjunct faculty? Are there special issues surrounding the use of faculty for credit versus noncredit courses?

Budget constraints, decreasing state support, retirements, and changing enrollment patterns all play a role in the need for adjuncts. In addition, adjuncts provide a buffer for full-time faculty. In many academic areas, decreases in enrollment affect the hiring and use of part-time faculty before they impinge on full-time faculty jobs. This buffer is a welcomed practice for full-time faculty as long as they are satisfied with the ratio of full-time to part-time faculty. Adjuncts usually fill the need for the abundance in lower-level general education classes as well as specialized classes where there are few full-time faculty.

The growth of online programs, hybrid courses, and laboratory courses is also changing the role of faculty. Questions concerning office hours and class time are causing institutions to rethink the relationship between faculty and students. Institutions can use the talents, connections, and skills of adjuncts by tapping into their experiences to assist in developing curriculum, providing internships, tutoring, and serving on advisory councils.

Students also appreciate the fact that many adjuncts are practitioners who pepper their classroom lectures with real-world experiences. The connections to the community that adjuncts bring with them improve the reputation of the college and provide internships and job opportunities for students. Adjuncts also have the potential to add to the diversity of the institution's culture. Who better to teach in the fire administration program than the fire chief? Who better to teach in the criminal justice program than the police chief? The connection to the world of work cannot be stressed enough. Adjuncts have a special ability to bring life to ideas with interesting and often contemporary examples.

The Adjunct's Perspective

Scholars and practitioners become adjunct faculty for a number of reasons. Some want to earn extra money, whereas others find intrinsic satisfaction in giving back to the community and future generations. There are retired professionals seeking to remain active; for them, the position provides intellectual stimulation. Others serve as adjuncts in the hope that they will be hired for a tenure-track position. Still others teach because they enjoy the time spent at the college as time away from their children when they can mix with other adults. For these faculty members, a part-time job is just what they want.

Teaching loads for adjuncts usually range from one to three courses a semester. Over 50 percent of community college adjuncts teach two or more sections each term (Gappa, Austin, and Trice, 2007). Many have long-running relationships with institutions but recognize they will be paid less than full-time faculty and have little job security. Most adjunct faculty make less than three thousand dollars per course (Townsend, 2003). Market competitiveness usually determines the rate of adjunct pay. In urban areas, there is greater demand for adjuncts, causing the pay rate to be higher.

While many part-time faculty members enjoy their work, some feel disconnected and unappreciated. They show up at night when all the regular staff are gone and proceed to their classroom. Those who teach during the day are often forced to run in the building just in time to go to class and run back out, sometimes to another class at another institution. Given the literature that suggests that adjunct faculty need to feel a part of the intellectual life of the campus (Gappa, Austin, and Trice, 2007), colleges need to create ways for full-time and part-time faculty to work with and engage one another.

The lack of benefits is another major concern for adjunct faculty members. Many part-time faculty argue that they are doing the same job as their full-time counterparts but are not being paid fairly. Of equal concern, some note that they have the same level of education and the same years of experience as full-time faculty.

The Question of Quality

There are very important and complex challenges when measuring the quality of adjunct faculty members. Who has defined the institutional standards and expected student outcomes? Who provides oversight? Do adjuncts have the proper experiences to relate to community college students and colleagues? What about academic credentials? Do adjuncts know how to connect students to resources? When adjuncts teach online, what constitutes the difference of work between adjuncts and full-timers? All of these questions are of concern to college presidents and chief academic officers. So how do they approach the questions while maintaining academic quality?

To ensure a good fit between part-time faculty and the institution, the academic vice president or dean must have hiring and training procedures in place. Being very clear about the desired credentials and instruction needs helps in developing methods used to find and acquire the proper adjunct faculty. The quality of thought that goes into the advertising is the first indication of the expectations and standards set by the institution. From this point on, every contact reveals the values and expectations of the institution and division. A proper orientation to the institution and opportunities for continuing development are of critical value.

After the hiring process, the supervising administrator must continue to examine the adjunct's syllabus and other materials. Monitoring these materials will provide the clearest indication as to whether the faculty member is in sync with the institutional mission. Close monitoring of key materials provides the best insight into what is happening between teacher and students. The monitoring must be set in policy and practices—and then closely watched. When these practices are institutionalized, administrators can feel some comfort in the level of quality of both full-time and part-time faculty.

There are also many duties required of full-time faculty that adjuncts are not expected to perform. Full-time faculty usually provide office hours, work on curriculum, and serve on search committees. However, many adjuncts wish to perform these duties as a way to feel connected to the institution. In order for adjuncts to participate, there must be opportunities for their development so that their participation can be meaningful. Adjuncts can provide good information on the value of the institution's orientation and hiring process. This information is easily attained yet rarely acquired. In addition, adjuncts can provide unique insight into hiring committees.

Advising and counseling are complex issues for faculty due to the individualized nature and skill sets needed to be of assistance. Counseling is best left to the professionals, who are properly trained to address student needs. Nonetheless, adjuncts as well as full-time faculty need to be aware of services available to students and should be able to provide information to students when approached. Given advances in technology, adjuncts should be able to access most programmatic information online and therefore answer student questions.

The question of the quality of adjuncts and their relationship to institutional governance is another complex issue. Some institutional leaders believe that adjuncts should have an active role in governance, while others believe their duties lie solely in the classroom. Most of the significant issues involving adjuncts and governance are found in institutions where there is an adjunct union. This situation can be complicated by the fact that administrators must deal with the full-time union and the adjunct union, especially if the relationship between the two organizations is strained. Having insightful supervisors who deal professionally with adjuncts can assist the institution in maintaining relationships by including them in discussions about instructional quality and student outcomes and integrating their concerns into the fabric of the college's development.

The quality of part-time faculty members' teaching is always a significant issue for administrators. The research in this area shows no significant difference between full-time and part-time faculty. Nonetheless, questions of quality will continue to be asked as the role of faculty changes due to online and hybrid instruction as well as the use of individualized diagnostic and prescriptive software.

Finally, having adjuncts perform duties other than teaching should be done carefully. Full-time faculty will question the practice, as will other staff. However, this should not stop an institution from making use of part-time faculty members' valuable services and talents. The key to acquiring such services is in the process used to acquire the service. Having a team of full-time and part-time faculty address an issue together can be a valuable practice and pay big dividends for both the institution and the faculty. Supervisors should be cognizant of opportunities throughout the year when adjuncts can play a role in the intellectual culture of the institution and then organize the participation to maximize the benefit.

Finding Quality Adjuncts

Finding adjuncts encompasses many factors: location, institutional need, timing, and the availability of positions on other campuses. When hiring adjuncts, administrators must understand that communication of the institution's values begins with the first contact, which may be with an employee of the college or an advertisement in a newspaper. Everything thereafter will also send a message about the standards of the institution. Having a systematic hiring approach provides the hiring dean the opportunity to spend meaningful time with each prospective teacher. Taking time at the beginning of the process also provides the dean with greater flexibility and allows him or her to form a relationship with the adjunct, who most likely is looking at all available positions, including those at other colleges and universities.

Administrators should also look to practicing and retired professionals, who bring value to the institution because of their advanced experience and knowledge. Former faculty members bring a wealth of information about how the institution functions and can be useful in assisting with other adjuncts. Because of the high rate at which faculty are retiring, many colleges are creating special emeritus programs to keep faculty involved.

Competition for adjuncts no longer comes only from other institutions in the local area. Institutions that have large online programs now compete with institutions around the world. Community colleges also have to compete for adjuncts with other community colleges and universities. Competing with four-year institutions can be difficult because the teaching demands are greater at the community college.

Becoming Part of the Fabric of the Institution

Administrators must invest in and embrace adjunct faculty as a critical part of the culture. When considering integrating adjuncts into the institution, ongoing professional development becomes critical. Administrators should meet regularly with part-time faculty to discuss institutional mission, service to students, academic values, and the use of technology. Adjuncts also need to be aware of the changing higher education landscape, faculty roles, student diversity, changing demands of the world of work, and demands for increased accountability.

Finally, the insightful administrator must recognize that adjunct faculty members are diverse in terms of the amount and type of institutional development and support needed. Part-time faculty come with various lifestyles and reasons for being an adjunct. The hiring administrator must get to know potential adjuncts in reference to their abilities to work with students and other faculty. The administrator must also determine if the adjuncts will be reliable long-term employees as well as observe how they approach the institution's expectations for continuing development.

From First Interview to Orientation. Based on my own experiences as a part-time faculty member and an academic administrator, I believe the community college should do more to orientate faculty. The hiring administrator should have a checklist with important questions to ask at each interview. The information derived will assist greatly in planning a proper orientation. Expectations must be established at once. Time should be set aside to review the faculty handbook, complete the necessary paperwork, and introduce the adjunct to full-time faculty, other adjuncts, and staff members. Making these activities mandatory and explaining the vision and passion the institution has for such activities sends a strong message to adjuncts.

All orientations or training should begin with a discussion of the mission and values, the importance of student growth, and the relationship between the college and the larger community. Next, all the important yet more mundane issues need to be discussed: personnel matters, organizational structure, instructional components, and administrative policies and procedures. It is useful to provide faculty with written copies of all such information. Finally, faculty should know how and when they will be evaluated by students and the institution. To recap, the key to the first meeting is to welcome part-time faculty, provide critical information about getting ready, and introduce them to the institutional philosophy and campus resources.

Practical Support. Institutional support for adjunct faculty members varies greatly. Some have no office, clerical support, or connection to other faculty; others have access to e-mail, an office, and administrative support, and they are mentored by full-time faculty members. When thinking about the support institutions provide, administrators should consider the following questions: Do adjuncts need keys? Do they need identification cards, business cards, or decals for parking? Are they included in institutional events and celebrations? Then consider more complex issues like academic freedom, instructional design, and technology.

Regardless of the more esoteric questions of the academy, there are basic informational items that all adjuncts need to know: syllabi requirements, class times, student assessment and feedback requirements, grading policies, attendance policies, classroom management policies, time lines for grades and grade input, add and drop procedures, plagiarism policy, the availability of technical assistance, the location of student services, and the selection of texts and other materials.

Hiring administrators at multicampus colleges also need to make a special effort to communicate with each other about adjunct faculty who may shop around for the best classes at the best times. This often causes an administrator to lose an adjunct because another campus offers a class at a better time. Remember that if you are the administrator who wins this semester, you could be the loser next semester. Adjuncts will notice that there are no matching standards from campus to campus. Again, this is a good reason for deans to share information and model course materials.

The Need for Ongoing Development. It has been a standard in higher education for faculty to focus on disciplinary competence, not on pedagogy. Sadly, many faculty begin the process of teaching with little knowledge about teaching, unless, of course, the faculty member has taught in a high school. Therefore, the college should work to create instructional development training for part-time faculty. Development activities need to be in sync with the changing role of the faculty, the changing student body, and changing technology. The development of adjuncts should be an ongoing goal, just as it is with full-timers. However, care must be taken in providing opportunities in recognition of time and financial constraints. When is the best time for an institution to offer development opportunities, and under what conditions? Administrators should be thoughtful about subject area content, instructional design that includes the latest technology, and the enhancement of relationships.

Other staff at the institution will analyze how much an institution invests in adjuncts. How will the full-time faculty react to spending institutional funds on adjuncts? How will the staff react? Do you offer the same opportunities at the same times? How do you communicate opportunities? Do you pay for developmental costs and pay the adjuncts for being developed? Answers to these questions are a direct indication of the value put on adjunct faculty in reference to monetary resources and thoughtfulness.

Areas Critical to Adjunct Development. When beginning the discussion of development with an adjunct, start with the mission. Have a card with the institutional goals, go over the goals, and explain that all actions of the institution reflect these goals. Adjuncts need to understand the goals and realize that they are instruments in bringing the goals to fruition. If they are uncomfortable with the goals, the hiring supervisor needs to know immediately. Critical conversations need to take place with adjuncts; it is only through this conversation that the hiring administrator will be able to judge the fit of adjuncts to the institution.

The First Day and the First Week. We have all heard stories of the instructor who asks students to look to the left and then to the right and understand that one of those seen will soon disappear from the course. This type of attitude should not be tolerated. Adjuncts need to know that the first day is critical in setting the foundation for student success. Developing a relationship for learning begins immediately; assist adjuncts in developing strategies to maximize the positive messages sent the first day. In addition, have them conceptualize the first week. If possible, have adjuncts sit in on the first class of one of the institution's best teachers. If a dean or chair has a line of students waiting at the door to drop the course, you can bet there was a problem that could have been avoided with a proper orientation.

Student Contact and Interaction. Adjuncts need to know what types of interactions are expected. Are there office hours? Where do they hold office hours if they have no office? Does the institution encourage faculty to invite students to their homes? Is having office hours at home by e-mail an accepted practice? Discussing these questions is important and may help avoid difficulties throughout the semester.

Cooperative Learning. Research has shown clearly that students learn from other students. However, there are techniques to be learned if adjuncts are to maximize the power of others in the class.

Student Outcomes, Assessment, and Feedback. It is critical that part-time faculty members be clear about student outcomes and course objectives and include appropriate assessment and feedback. Encouraging adjuncts and helping them understand that assessment and feedback are teaching tools is important. Feedback should be part of the teaching process, not a hammer held over students to force compliance. Furthermore, assessments and feedback must be timely, comprehensive, and meaningful in relation to further learning.

Relevance. How often have we heard the question about why something needs to be learned when it appears to have no relevance? Adjuncts need to understand that students seek relevance in what they learn. This transition from complex, abstract concepts to everyday life is not easy. Teachers must continually seek new and contemporary examples for students. Bringing in professionals who can assist faculty in their specialized areas can be of great assistance. Making material relevant is easier when students are active learners instead of passive receivers.

Pace of Instruction. Knowing how to judge the pace of a course is a complex challenge for those who are new or inexperienced. Helping adjuncts learn how to analyze their pace of instruction can go a long way in helping them be successful. In addition, administrators should help adjuncts understand that the complexity of interactions is related to pace and needs to be planned carefully and built in such a way as to allow individualization.

Emotions and Senses. When we are young, we learn to solve problems in a world full of complex challenges. All of our senses and emotions are fully engaged. However, in college, we often become passive listeners, jarred awake only when the time to move to the next class arrives. To address this, adjuncts need to learn how to fully engage students and use the sophisticated technology available to stimulate all senses.

Teacher Enthusiasm. The emotional level of the teacher will have an impact on the level of excitement in the classroom. Adjuncts who love their discipline and are enthusiastic about it will approach the art of teaching in a much different way than will an adjunct who is going through the motions. It is important to visit the classroom to observe the emotional level in the class.

Teacher as Model. Teachers model the behaviors that the institution expects and values. The future is now in reference to using technology to enhance pedagogy. Adjunct faculty should know and understand the value and proper use of interactive technologies and computer applications, and their relationship to student motivation and learning.

Evaluations. Adjunct evaluations are usually made up of two components: visits to a class once a semester and student evaluations. Visiting a classroom once is for the most part an unproductive use of time yet remains a common practice. The only way to get an idea of ongoing class interaction is to visit multiple times under varying conditions. This is also the case for hybrid and online "visits." The supervising administrator needs to look at grade distributions and, most of all, syllabi, tone, and quality of assignments. Listen to other faculty and students; rumors can actually serve as an indication that a closer look is needed. Make sure to provide personal feedback on all areas.

Ask full-time faculty to provide guidance and share materials. Ask other faculty to go to classes and invite adjuncts to their classes. Supervisors have the luxury to end the association with most adjuncts at will. Be sure to know if a written evaluation is needed. Agreements with unions may have an impact, as will the contract signed by the adjunct. When possible, have a personal discussion about the areas of concern and areas of excellence. Adjuncts are in a tenuous position concerning their relationship with the college and students. They desire to do a good job and need support and encouragement. Provide awards and recognition to adjuncts, for they are a critical component of most institutions of higher education.

Maintaining Institutional Standards: A Creative Solution

The demand for accountability in terms of student learning outcomes continues to gain momentum. Academic leaders put a great deal of trust in the faculty to deliver instruction that results in a high level of student learning outcomes. However, if full- and part-time faculty were asked to identify the learning outcomes and present the data documenting common results, one would likely receive little data. College faculty are not well versed at specifying outcomes or assessment measures This situation is being highlighted by accrediting agencies in reference to general education outcomes, departmental outcomes, and specific course outcomes. If an institution has a hundred beginning psychology faculty teaching a hundred introduction to psychology courses, there will be a hundred different courses, resulting in a great variety of student learning outcomes. Having a variety of pedagogy, styles, and methods of delivery is not the issue. The issue lies in two basic questions: Does your psychology department have standards of student learning? If so, what are they, and how does the department know that the standards are being maintained?

What if, as an academic leader, you had full confidence that all adjuncts were given materials in which the academic standards developed by the full-time faculty were embedded, including specific learning outcomes? In addition, all adjuncts were provided assessments that were properly correlated with specific learning outcomes and timed in reference to being proctored to maximize individual learning styles and rates. Adjuncts were given units of instruction that matched the learning outcomes and assessments. And finally, the materials provided were but a foundation, leaving plenty of room for the adjunct to express his or her individuality while still maintaining the departmental standards.

Florida Community College at Jacksonville has embarked on a project in cooperation with McGraw-Hill for the development of course materials in standard general education courses. The project, named Sirius Academics, is elaborated on by a professor at the college, Kathleen Ciez-Volz (2006): "Sirius Academics encompasses the redesign of developmental and college-credit courses" that experience both high enrollment and high attrition. The initiative "couples innovative instructional design with engaging multimedia . . . to create optimal learning environments in which students interact with one another, the instructor, and course content." Ciez-Volz explains that the course materials are developed by members of each department and include a text, CD-ROM, and a completed online platform. The combined materials for the complete course wholesale for fifty dollars—much less than usual class-required materials.

In my first experience as an adjunct, my students and I would have had a much better experience if I had been able to use materials like those identified by Ciez-Volz. I believe the future will involve the full-time faculty identifying discipline-based student learning outcomes and that materials will be developed and shared with the adjuncts to help ensure that student outcomes have indeed been identified and are being assessed. Here is a new path for institutions pursuing the continuing quest for quality among adjunct faculty.

References

Berger, A., Kirshstein, R., Zhang, Y., and Carter, K. *A Profile of Part-Time Faculty.* Washington, D.C.: U.S. Department of Education, 2002.

Ciez-Volz, K. "Within a Star's Reach: The Sirius Academic Initiative." *NISOD Innovation Abstracts,* 2006, 28(7), 2006.

Gappa, J. M., Austin, A. E., and Trice, A. G. *Rethinking Faculty Work.* San Francisco: Jossey-Bass, 2007.

Maeroff, G. *A Classroom of One: How Online Learning Is Changing Our Schools and Colleges.* New York: Palgrave, 2003.

Townsend, B. "Changing Relationships, Changing Values in the American Classroom." In E. Benjamin (ed.), *Exploring the Role of Contingent Instructional Staff in Undergraduate Learning.* New Directions for Higher Education, no. 123. San Francisco: Jossey Bass, 2003.

U.S. Department of Education. *National Study of Postsecondary Faculty.* Washington, D.C.: U.S. Department of Education, 2003.

DONALD W. GREEN *is the executive vice president for instruction and student services at Florida Community College at Jacksonville.*

5

This chapter highlights some issues that are being addressed, discussed, and analyzed by part-time faculty in the California Community College system.

Part-Time Faculty in California: Successes, Challenges, and Future Issues

Robert B. Yoshioka

The year 2007 marks forty years of indentured servitude on the part of part-time faculty teaching in the California Community College system. Approximately forty thousand dedicated, highly trained, and motivated teachers work alongside twelve thousand tenured full-time faculty. Sadly, for all their efforts, part-time faculty members receive little recognition for their work and sacrifice. While student success and the challenges posed by a growing and diverse population should be paramount, part-time faculty devote much of their day to matters of personal economic survival.

In order to understand the plight of part-time faculty in California, it is necessary to provide the historical and legislative context within which part-timers find themselves today. This is particularly important considering that the California Community College system cannot provide students with the finest educational opportunities when more than two-thirds of its instructors are underpaid and overworked. Based on my experiences as a part-time faculty member and union organizer, I discuss three key pieces of California legislation that have significant implications for part-time faculty. I then illustrate how part-time faculty have worked to improve their employment conditions.

The Part-Time Faculty Members' Legislative House of Cards

Over the past forty years, the California State Legislature has enacted three pieces of legislation—Senate Bill 316 (1967), Assembly Bill 1725 (1989), and Assembly Bill 420 (1999)—that have collectively resulted in the creation, maintenance, and oppression of part-time faculty within the California Community College system.

SB 316 allowed community college districts to hire temporary, nontenure-track faculty to teach on a limited basis as a reasonable augmentation to full-time tenure-track faculty. This legislation allowed community colleges to take advantage of federal funding that was directed toward higher education. Hiring temporary faculty as hourly employees rather than as tenure-track instructors allowed community colleges to cash in on federal grant programs without creating a cadre of tenure-track faculty who might bankrupt the system when the extramural funding ended. In addition, the legislation stipulated that these hourly teachers could not become probationary employees if they taught less than 60 percent of a full-time assignment. This is the origin of the now infamous 60 percent law, which prevents part-time faculty members from acquiring more than a 60 percent course load at any single college.

The 60 percent law was promulgated without a sunset clause; that is, the law did not have a predetermined termination date. This loophole effectively created an open-ended and highly lucrative way for community college administrators to exploit this newly created underclass of part-time faculty. Part-timers became the institutional actors who allow community colleges to provide more and cheaper educational services to an increasingly large number of students.

AB 1725 mandated that 75 percent of all community college classes were to be taught by full-time faculty, with the remaining 25 percent of classes taught by part-time faculty. Unfortunately, this legislation was heavy on intent and light on compliance language, and districts were quick to find ways around this mandated requirement. The net result was the consistent appeals of community college administrators for exemptions, postponements, and forgiveness for their inability to make reasonable progress toward instituting the 75:25 ratio. Although some districts made significant progress toward or already meet the 75:25 ratio, overall instructional ratios have not varied by more than two or three percentage points in the past eighteen years (Workgroup on 75–25 Issues, 2005). This lack of meaningful movement toward hiring more full-time faculty has a direct impact on the growing number of part-time faculty who are recruited to teach more and more classes.

AB 420 was designed to bring moderate relief to part-time faculty by providing paid office hours, minimal health benefits, and parity pay. Again, the bill was strong on intent language and weak on compliance. For example, locally bargained benefits resulted in seventy-three different definitions of *parity*, only a few of which provided at least 89 percent of the compensation that full-time faculty receive for the same work.

Although a few districts with parity pay at 100 percent, current systemwide record keeping is in such disarray that the 2006–2007 report on parity will not be published because districts are unable to accurately report their current distribution of mandated state funds for parity. Some districts have not negotiated a definition for *parity* and have not distributed any of the mandated funds to part-time faculty. Of equal concern are other districts that have routinely given parity money to full-time faculty who teach overload classes. The abuse is so great in one district that 47 percent of parity funds were diverted to pay full-time faculty who taught overload classes.

Districts are loath to support legitimate requests for system-mandated health care benefits. Most districts are unwilling to pay for these benefits for part-time faculty, arguing that these expenses would raise the cost of employing part-time faculty. District commitment to part-time health care can be callous and unfeeling; many of our number are simply told, "Don't get sick while teaching!"

There is also a situation surrounding paid office hours and dedicated space (offices) in which to hold office hours. Districts are realizing that making it possible for part-time faculty to regularly meet with their students is a necessary and essential part of the educational process. Yet many districts do not provide dedicated space for offices and do not pay part-time faculty to hold office hours.

Professionalism would dictate that teachers regularly meet with their students outside class. Many part-time faculty members resort to meeting with their students in the student union, in restaurants, outside, and even in their cars. Although administrators deplore this turn of events, part-timers are rarely found on campus between classes. Absence from campus not only has a deleterious effect on students, but also prevents many part-time faculty from participating in campus life and culture.

To recap, economic uncertainty, little or no job security, low pay, inadequate health benefits, and minimal paid office hours all contribute to the shocking 20 to 25 percent annual turnover of part-time faculty (Goldstein, Yoshioka, and Baringer, 2005). Just stabilizing the part-time workforce would be a major achievement, yet administrators treat part-time faculty as an endlessly renewable resource.

The Internet: Part-Time Faculty Members' New Lifeline

The founding of the California Part-Time Faculty Association (CPFA) was facilitated by access to the Internet, an unprecedented organizing tool. It became possible to reach out to part-time faculty on each of the 109 campuses within the community college system. While webmasters on some campuses guarded access to faculty e-mail accounts, it soon became easy to locate and communicate with other part-time faculty who had been isolated and alienated. The Internet also allows CPFA to send out electronic litera-ture to its membership quickly and efficiently. This is not to say that open access is a panacea; it is not. Yet we would not have been able to organize, mobilize, or lobby as effectively if we were not able to access the Internet.

CPFA originated and continues to maintain an active, open, subscription-based listserv for its members. Our membership is drawn from all education unions and even includes sympathetic full-time faculty and college adminis-trators, as well as members of the state legislature and the state chancellor's office. This electronic lifeline has enabled part-timers to keep informed on local, regional, and statewide issues that have a direct impact on their lives. Being able to rapidly gauge the impact of proposed legislation or new policies and being able to play a role in the policy process has been a great help to the organization.

Of course, there is a downside to the Internet for part-time faculty: online courses. With few exceptions, districts around the state encourage part-time faculty to develop online classes. However, until recently, districts found myriad ways to avoid paying part-time faculty for this course devel-opment. As it stands, few districts pay part-timers for developing online courses, arguing that additional payment would place them over their 60 per-cent load limitations. So part-timers who think that volunteering to develop online courses without compensation might lead to favorable consideration for full-time positions are coerced into working. Moreover, when the course development is complete, there is no guarantee that the part-time faculty member will be able to teach that course because the software company that has been contracted by the district to support online education also owns the course and content. Districts and the software vendors are then free to mar-ket the course and its contents regionally, nationally, or internationally.

In contrast, full-time faculty members who participate in online course development are paid well for their initial efforts and retain some intellec-tual property rights to their work. Compensation rates roughly mirror the disparity between full-time and part-time hourly rates. Short of removing the economic incentives for hiring and retaining part-time faculty, there is little reason for districts, unions, and full-time faculty to address the eco-nomic exploitation of part-time faculty in the community colleges.

Proximity Is Destiny

One of the best ways to ensure student success is for students to have timely and frequent access to their teachers. In this respect, part-time faculty are caught in the jaws of a monumental dilemma. Many want to spend time with students in order to help them succeed. However, because part-time faculty are prohibited from teaching more than 60 percent of a load on any one cam-pus, many have to become "freeway flyers" in order to make a modest living.

Although administrators and full-time faculty do not expect part-time faculty to remain on campus after their classes are over, many part-timers believe that donating their free time to extracurricular activities and tutoring will increase their chances of obtaining a full-time position. In fact, administrators and full-time faculty laud part-time volunteerism, but say in the same breath that they themselves would not make that kind of sacrifice.

On any community college campus, one is likely to find part-timers chatting with their students in the hallways, in the campus commons, or outdoors in their cars. While these part-time faculty members are well intentioned, they are helping to perpetuate the exploitation of their profession. Student success is purchased with part-time faculty donations of their time outside class. Yes, students get the best of what part-time faculty have to give, but the price that these hours exact is merely a stopgap that fails to address the underlying problem of the overuse of underpaid teaching professionals.

New Rules, New Game

CPFA is in a unique position to provide all part-time faculty with a safe haven and nonjudgmental public forum in which to clarify issues and craft policies. Until part-time faculty members create an effective advocacy group, they will be relegated to second-class status in their various unions. While the plight and economic exploitation of part-time faculty are often spoken of, little progress has been made toward remediating these abuses. Although the concerns of part-timers were often included as openers by union negotiating teams, they tended to be removed from the table once bargaining for full-time contract provisions was successfully completed.

Slowly things began to change as part-time faculty were successful in creating bargaining units sometimes within, but often outside, the negotiating teams fielded by the full-time faculty. These exercises began to empower and then embolden part-time activists to press successfully for greater change and more concessions. As part-time faculty gains began to increase, more and more of us began to believe that significant change was possible. To that end, we began the difficult and uncomfortable processes of self-examination and redefinition. Out of that continuing dialogue has come a vision of the future that is more aggressive and self-directed, even to the extent of renaming ourselves and looking creatively at ways to save the community college from itself.

What's in a Name?

Names such as *part-time faculty, adjunct faculty,* and *contingent laborer* do not carry with them perceived status or positive connotations. In fact, one can make an argument that such terms are euphemistic, given to us in order to immediately identify our second-class status. I believe that we are at a point in our consciousness raising where self-naming becomes critical to our development of a positive group identity. It does not much matter what we call ourselves, as long as it is a name that we give ourselves.

A cloud of new names brings new insight to who we are and what we want. It is a significant step toward reclaiming our dignity as well as giving ourselves power over who we are and how we wish to be perceived. One new name that now figures prominently is *non-tenure-track temporary employees* (NTTTE). NTTTE does not come with any emotional baggage or carry with it any negative connotations. It is a name that we choose to give ourselves and will probably be changed as the need arises.

This naming process will have an impact on how we frame future issues and respond to future pressures. Equally important is our growing ability to enter into the political arena to solve some of our problems by seeking sponsorship for our own legislation. Turning our concerns into binding legislation will allow us to craft solutions that solve some of the major staffing and quality issues in the community colleges.

After the passage of AB 420 in 1999, most part-time faculty returned to the classroom, content in the belief that we had won a major political victory. Over the ensuing eight years, however, it has become painfully clear that our gains have been eroded by relentless attacks, noncompliance, and outright refusal to implement sections of the law. We are now back in the legislative trenches working on legislation that we hope will fix the system and result in parity and equity for NTTTE.

Our Future Writ Large

Unions, faculty associations, higher education consortia, and even CPFA all have legislation pending in California. Why is there so much activity? What is at stake? What needs to be changed?

In a major initiative, every possible interest group (except for CPFA) is mounting an attack demanding that more full-time faculty be hired. Nevertheless, AB 591 is written by and for NTTTEs and focuses on remediating NTTTE exploitation. This legislation calls for us to teach a 100 percent load, reach parity in two years, and receive comparable health benefits. Finally, it mandates hiring at least 50 percent of all new and replacement full-time positions from a pool of qualified NTTTEs from around the state. No other bills currently under active consideration put NTTTE interests first.

There will continue to be tenured and nontenured faculty teaching in the community colleges. Therefore, all faculty should be compensated according to the same criteria, the only difference being the terms of employment. Removing the artificial barriers and minimizing the differences between members of these two groups of equally qualified teachers will have the net result of leveling the playing field and will substantially improve the quality of education available to all students we teach.

NEW DIRECTIONS FOR COMMUNITY COLLEGES • DOI: 10.1002/cc

Neither administrators nor full-time tenured faculty have tried to stem the use of exploited NTTTEs from flooding academe. NTTTEs did not cause this problem but are blamed for it. If we do not begin to make significant progress toward regularizing and reprofessionalizing faculty ranks, our schools will continue to decline and the quality of our graduates will also fall. Legislative remedy is the next battleground for NTTTEs. We must be willing to take the battle to the heart of our government when seeking economic relief and social justice. This is the state of affairs as we see it; these are our issues and our challenges. What will the future hold for NTTTEs? Victory, of course

References

Goldstein, M. M., Yoshioka, R., and Baringer, S. *California Part-Time Faculty Association Frequently Asked Questions on the 60–80 Percent Law Change.* Santa Monica: California Part-Time Faculty Association, 2005.

Workgroup on 75–25 Issues. *Report and Recommendations.* Sacramento: California Community Colleges Chancellor's Office, 2005.

ROBERT B. YOSHIOKA *is a recently retired community college non-tenure-track temporary employee, union activist, and cofounder of the California Part-Time Faculty Association.*

6

This chapter explores recent legal challenges and victories brought forth by part-time community college faculty in Washington State in an effort to attain equity and social justice.

The Stone That Struck Goliath: The Part-Time Faculty Association, Washington State Community and Technical Colleges, and Class-Action Lawsuits

Eddy A. Ruiz

In August 1996, a three-part series of Gary Trudeau's *Doonesbury* cartoons portrayed the growing plight of faculty tenure and the increasing reliance on part-time faculty. The comic depicts a college president who inquires about the institution's budget, which had been in the red, only to find that it is now running a surplus because of tuition hikes and abandonment of tenure. The president's assistant assures him the college can still attract competent faculty. A crowd gathers for an adjunct auction in response to the institution's need for two romantic literature instructors. The bidding begins. A potential adjunct candidate cries out that he holds a doctorate from Cornell University, does not expect tenure, and would like a two-year contract, medical benefits, and three months severance. With megaphone in hand, the auctioneer ignores the offer and continues the search. Another potential candidate shouts that he would be willing to work for food. In the last comic strip, the college asks for a Keynesian economist. An individual among the crowd raises his hand and says he requires only that the institution provide a living wage and treat him like a human being. The auctioneer turns away to continue the search only to have the candidate recant the plea to be treated like a human being. Although the Doonesbury piece is

NEW DIRECTIONS FOR COMMUNITY COLLEGES, no. 140, Winter 2007 © 2007 Wiley Periodicals, Inc.
Published online in Wiley InterScience (www.interscience.wiley.com) • DOI: 10.1002/cc.304

satirical, it highlights the growing reliance on adjunct faculty and their plight.

Higher education is dealing with an increased demand for access and accountability, a tight job market, complaints that teaching is secondary to research, and a focus on hiring part-time instructors (Duncan, 1999). As it stands, 526,000 full- and part-time faculty members comprise the academy (Altbach, 2005). Part-time faculty have become increasingly attractive to colleges and universities because they cost less, provide flexibility, and are expendable. Just as in corporate America, pensions and employment longevity are rapidly becoming a thing of the past as thousands of workers are displaced and professions are outsourced to more cost-efficient countries. In higher education, part-time faculty teach 40 percent of all higher education classes. Between 1970 and 2000, adjunct employees grew from 20 percent to 64 percent of the academic workforce at community colleges (Longmate and Cosco, 2002); this is a group that the U.S. Department of Labor considers part time despite the reality that they can and often do work forty or more hours per week (Duncan, 1999).

Some business and professional employees apply for adjunct community college positions to provide esoteric knowledge or highly specialized skills to students; others enjoy the flexibility, freedom, and noncommittal nature of part-time employment; and still others seek permanent work and are exploited. Cohen and Brawer (2003) note that administrators rationalize the exploitation because part-time faculty are cheaper on a per class basis. In California, community college adjuncts receive $2,000 for a sixteen-week, three-unit course, and in Illinois the rate is $1,224. In contrast, their full-time counterparts earn up to three times more. This growing reliance on part-time faculty influences work conditions, institutional integration, and organizational culture as two-year institutions willingly exploit the academic labor market (Wagoner, Metcalfe, and Olaore, 2005).

In Washington State, part-time community college faculty outnumber full-time instructors by three to one, teach 50 percent of all classes, and earn only 40 percent of what full-time faculty make. Of equal concern, 83 percent receive no health benefits, and 87.5 percent receive no retirement benefits. These statistics, however, do not imply that adjunct faculty members are powerless. Members of the Part-Time Faculty Association of Washington State Community and Technical Colleges have refused to accept this second-class citizen status and fought back with the use of class-action litigation to address worker exploitation in the community college system. This legal brinkmanship is uncommon but speaks to the issues that temporary faculty face in nearly every state. This chapter reports on the recent events surrounding the Part-Time Faculty Association, the contentious environment of faculty unions, the nature of the lawsuits brought against the state of Washington, and the results of that class action litigation.

NEW DIRECTIONS FOR COMMUNITY COLLEGES • DOI: 10.1002/cc

Union Tensions

In 1998, the American Federation of Teachers of Washington, the Washington Education Association, and the State Board for Community and Technical Colleges published the *Best Practices Task Force Report* to rally adjunct instructors and gain the support of full-time faculty. The platform centered on the issue of part-time faculty equity. This collective political action lobbied Washington State legislatures in an effort to highlight an inherent double standard within the community college system: earnings and benefits. As in other states, the average salary for community college adjuncts was significantly below that of their tenured peers despite teaching the same classes. Small inroads were made. Working together, the faculty labor unions were able to increase the part-time instructor pay scale from forty to sixty cents on the dollar. Those who worked more than half time began to receive full benefits and prorated retirement benefits. In addition, unemployment rules were expanded for adjunct instructors because they did not receive any guarantee of future employment by their current institution (Schroeder, 2005). At first, the gains appeared to be significant when considering the plight of some faculty. Nonetheless, a duel system of inequality remained (Cohen and Brawer, 2003); adjunct instructors were still denied equal pay for equal work. This inequality contributed to tension between the unions and the Part-Time Faculty Association.

Union leadership at the local, state, and national levels is heavily weighted in favor of full-time instructors. Within the American Federation of Teachers, only 17 of the 135 bargaining units are dedicated to part-time faculty. An obvious inequitable power dynamic exists that can limit the direction of lobbying, legislation, and salary distribution. In Washington State, thirty-four local unions obtained $15 million in raises between 1999 and 2004. However, only 10 percent went to adjunct faculty, who teach nearly half of all classes; 90 percent went to tenured faculty, who teach an equivalent number of classes (Hoeller, 2006). These raises were in addition to guaranteed retirement and health coverage benefits that full-timers receive. Hoeller (2006) notes that tenured faculty within the community college system are the bosses who hire and fire, decide who teaches and get raises, and determine which adjuncts are laid off. This inequitable structure relegates adjunct instructors to the status of indentured servants (Duncan, 1999). Moreover, this relationship affects union solidarity. Although the National Education Association has advocated prorated wages for part-time instructors since 1976, few faculty unions and higher education institutions have supported this practice (Longmate and Cosco, 2002). These factors underscore why the Part-Time Faculty Association has resisted the Washington American Federation of Teachers' goals and mandates.

Lawsuits and State Priorities

Members of the Part-Time Faculty Association of Washington Community and Technical Colleges have mobilized, defined their own agenda, and used class action lawsuits to challenge inequity. Since 1998, two separate class action suits regarding compensation, retirement, and health benefits have been filed in an effort to end academic exploitation. The defendant, the Washington community college system, denied any wrongdoing or exploitation, arguing that equal wages for adjuncts would cost the state $63 million. Earl Hale, executive director of the State Board for Community and Technical Colleges, noted that the motivation is not mean-spirited; rather, it is a reality of state budget allocation, as community colleges receive five hundred dollars less than high schools and fifteen hundred dollars less than four-year institutions on a per student basis (Lords, 1999).

In the first case, the plaintiffs contended that the community colleges had unfairly denied compensation in relation to overtime and out-of-class work (Lords, 1999). Previously, part-time instructors, in accord with the collective bargaining agreement, were considered eligible only for contract hours, barred from compensation for nonclassroom activities, and dubbed ineligible to receive overtime pay, unlike full-time faculty (Schneider, 2000). Although they were fully employed, part-time faculty would earn only seventeen thousand dollars annually due to their status. However, a key court ruling sided in favor of part-time instructors because the services rendered to students were not restricted to the classroom. An adjunct faculty member simply does not walk into class and serendipitously present the topic of the day to the students, vacate the premises, and repeat the process day-in and day-out without additional responsibilities or accountability. The delivery of instruction is only one component. Instructors develop curriculum; provide academic guidance after class, during office hours, and via e-mail; grade student assignments; and attend faculty meetings regardless of full- or part-time status (Euben, 2006).

In the second case, the plaintiffs argued that they were also disqualified from receiving health and retirement benefits. Eva Mader, a part-time German instructor and faculty member of Northern Seattle Community College for twenty-one consecutive years, and Teresa Knudson, who taught English for over ten years at the Community College of Spokane (Lords, 1999), argued that the state wrongfully denied its adjunct faculty retirement and health care benefits during the summer months. As a result, they felt that the state owed part-time faculty $40 million in back pay. In its decision, the Washington State Supreme Court ruled that the Health Care Authority improperly determined that part-time community college instructors were ineligible for health care coverage during summer by focusing on instructor titles rather than individual work circumstances when determining benefit eligibility. This class action suit was settled out of court for $12 million (Euben, 2006). The court's ruling extended beyond Mader and Knudson, and advanced the status of every other part-time Washington community college instructor in a similar predicament. These key rulings in regard to benefits and compensation are the result of bold actions taken by a few part-time faculty members, setting in motion the means by which to free themselves from their current second-class status in the community college system.

As a result of the class action lawsuit, Washington State community college adjunct faculty are now eligible to receive health coverage—during the summer months—if they teach at least 50 percent during the fall, winter, and spring quarters. Retirement also extends to part-time instructors who work half time or more. Furthermore, legislation is before the state senate to address community college staffing—the overuse of part-time faculty and full-time tenure attrition. The legislation seeks to increase the number of full-time tenure-track positions by 10 percent in each community college by 2013; raise salaries over and above a regular cost-of-living increase by 2013; attain prorated salary for adjunct instructors who have comparable qualifications and do comparable work; and grant adjuncts, after successful completion of a probationary period, a measure of job security through timely notice of next-term courses, priority consideration relating to teaching assignments, and the right of first refusal for eligible courses. The legislative goals are to improve the status of non-tenure-track faculty through equitable and comparable collective bargaining. The American Association of Universities and Professors has offered its public support and urged the American Federation of Teachers and the National Education Association to do likewise; both have refused to respond.

Conclusion

The Part-Time Faculty Association of Washington State Community and Technical Colleges, a small band of rebel adjunct instructors, has enacted its own agency to seek social justice. For years, adjuncts waited for the Goliath—faculty unions and the state—to address their pleas for equality and a living wage. Thus far, unions have attained raises of $15 million, but a 90:10 distribution of wealth tokenizes the role of adjuncts and is a move to placate the masses. The state too is culpable; it has viewed the exploitation of academic workers not as mean-spirited but rather as a means to save the state millions of dollars.

One possible blueprint to address adjunct inequality and exploitation is found in British Columbia. Its two- and four-year colleges operate under a collective agreement that maintains a prorated scale in relation to wages and faculty rights. Vancouver Community College faculty are not considered full- or part-time instructors. Rather, classification is based on successful completion of a two-year probationary period, whereby new professors are continually evaluated. Regardless of instructor location within the academic pipeline, they are paid on an equal prorated scale: an adjunct who works 50 to 75 percent receives half or three-quarters of the salary a full-time instructor earns who shares a similar pay grade. Second, part-time faculty accrue seniority on a prorated basis. Third, adjuncts receive benefits: professional development, vacation and sick leave, and medical and retirement coverage. Last, after successful completion of the probation period, part-time instructors automatically become regular faculty. This humanizing structure provides equal pay for equal work and creates solidarity (Longmate and Cosco, 2002).

The malicious neglect by some unions and Washington State has forced the hand of a few to defy the odds by using litigation to end a caste system. This nimble group has entered the fray despite facing Goliath and was rewarded with more equitable compensation and benefits. Aside from a social revolution the likes of which Marx called for, where workers of the world or, in this case, community college faculty, unite to overthrow the system, unions and state officials still have a window of opportunity to redeem themselves before future litigation becomes the norm in redressing academic inequality.

References

Altbach, P. G. "Harsh Realities: The Professorate Faces a New Century." In P. G. Altbach, R. O. Berdahl, and P. J. Gumport (eds.), *American Higher Education in the Twenty-First Century: Social, Political, and Economic Challenges.* Baltimore, Md.: Johns Hopkins University Press, 2005.
Cohen, A. M., and Brawer, F. B. *The American Community College.* (4th ed.) San Francisco: Jossey-Bass, 2003.
Duncan, J. C. "The Indentured Servants of Academia: The Adjunct Faculty Dilemma and Their Limited Legal Remedies." *Indiana Law Journal,* 1999, 74, 513–521.
Euben, D. "Legal Contingencies for Contingent Professors." *Chronicle of Higher Education,* Jun. 16, 2006, p. B8.
Hoeller, K. "The Proper Advocates for Adjuncts." *Chronicle of Higher Education,* June 16, 2006, p. B11.
Longmate, J., and Cosco, F. "Part-Time Instructors Deserve Equal Pay for Equal Work." *Chronicle of Higher Education,* May 3, 2002, p. B14.
Lords, E. "Part-Time Faculty Members Sue for Better Pay and Benefits." *Chronicle of Higher Education,* Apr. 2, 1999, p. A16.
Schneider, A. "Part-Time Faculty Members in Washington State Win Key Battle over Benefits." *Chronicle of Higher Education,* Feb. 25, 2000, p. A18.
Schroeder, S. "It's Time to Give Adjuncts a Break." *Chronicle of Higher Education,* Oct. 25. 2005, p. B26.
Wagoner, R. L., Metcalfe, A. S., and Olaore, I. "Fiscal Reality and Academic Quality: Part-Time Faculty and the Challenge to Organizational Culture at Community Colleges." *Community College Journal of Research and Practice,* 2005, 29, 1–20.
Washington State Board for Community and Technical Colleges. *Best Employment Practices for Part-Time Faculty.* Olympia: Washington State Board for Community and Technical Colleges, 2005.

EDDY A. RUIZ *is a doctoral student in higher education at the University of California, Los Angeles.*

7

Rio Salado is a nontraditional community college that is highly integrated in the global economy. This chapter describes the Rio Salado College systems approach, which relies almost exclusively on adjunct faculty to accomplish its mission, vision, and purposes.

A Systems Approach to Strategic Success with Adjunct Faculty

Vernon C. Smith

Rio Salado College has a reputation for being an innovative community college with a high reliance on adjunct faculty to accomplish its mission and purposes. A 2006 cover story for the *Chronicle for Higher Education* noted that only a few full-time faculty managed over a thousand adjuncts (Ashburn, 2006). Rio Salado College prides itself on its systems approach to the management of adjunct faculty. This approach directs faculty, organizational resources, personnel, and other supports so that adjunct faculty focus on teaching and learning processes—the core aspects of their work at the college. Davis, Helminski, and Smith (2005) and Bird (2006) have presented and shared some of the keys to this college's success. This chapter reviews and updates those strategies within the context of Rio Salado College's unique mission, vision, and culture. It also examines adjunct faculty as players and knowledge workers in the global economy.

Rio Salado College has what many would consider an ideal situation in terms of adjunct faculty at a community college. There is a stable, qualified, and proven cohort of adjunct faculty teaching courses. The adjunct faculty continue semester after semester, with little turnover. This stability has helped to maintain the quality and consistency of the instruction provided to students. The way Rio Salado successfully recruits, retains, evaluates, and manages adjunct faculty within a nontraditional academic context not only informs practitioners of best practices but also speaks to the nature of the adjunct faculty role in this new and challenging environment.

NEW DIRECTIONS FOR COMMUNITY COLLEGES, no. 140, Winter 2007 © 2007 Wiley Periodicals, Inc.
Published online in Wiley InterScience (www.interscience.wiley.com) • DOI: 10.1002/cc.305

Related Literature

Until recently, the literature on adjunct faculty in community colleges did not fully address the realities that Rio Salado College has encountered in its nearly thirty years of experience. In general, the use of adjunct faculty in institutions of higher education is increasing, especially in community colleges. Clery (1998) noted that between 1976 and 1995, the number of part-time faculty increased by 91 percent. By 1999, 65 percent of faculty at public two-year colleges were part time, whereas they formed 41 percent of faculty at private four-year colleges and 30 percent of faculty at public four-year institutions (U.S. Department of Education, 2003). Nationally, a new community college student is more likely to be taught by adjunct faculty than by a full-time faculty member.

Until recently scholarship on adjunct faculty has concentrated on two areas of investigation: the motivation and satisfaction of adjunct faculty and their effect on educational quality. Although both traditions acknowledge the fact that adjunct faculty numbers will continue to grow, they differ in their basic assumptions and attitudes about how and when to employ these faculty. Each advocates a preferred solution: avoid using adjunct faculty if at all possible, or help the adjunct faculty to fully participate through support, development, and unionization (Cason, Estep, and Hixson, 1999).

Whether they are described as invisible (Gappa and Leslie, 1993), strangers (Roueche, Roueche, and Milliron, 1995), the working poor, or accidental faculty (Gappa and Leslie, 1993), adjunct faculty have a lower-status position in the academic profession. Most adjunct faculty express some dissatisfaction with their status and working conditions (Roueche, Roueche, and Milliron, 1995). At the same time, they continue to be perceived as a threat to the profession because their tenuous status has led to the marginalization and disempowerment of full-time faculty (Cohen and Brawer, 2003; Rhoades, 1998).

This body of literature paints adjunct faculty as unable or unwilling to carry out their duties to an expected standard of quality. They are guilty, or guilty by association with perceptions of providing low-quality instruction, of being disconnected from the campus community and contributing to grade inflation (Sonner, 2000). While Roueche, Roueche, and Milliron (1995) argued that no significant study showed a difference in educational outcomes because of the use of adjunct faculty, there is now evidence that associates the number of adjunct faculty with lower graduation rates at community colleges (Jacoby, 2006).

In contrast to the negative view of adjunct faculty, it is clearly a benefit to community college students that adjunct faculty are more likely to have attended a community college themselves (Keim, 1989), acting as possible role models for increasingly diverse student populations. Moreover, community college adjunct faculty enjoy teaching and are committed. With this passion for teaching, they bring a real-world perspective grounded in

NEW DIRECTIONS FOR COMMUNITY COLLEGES • DOI: 10.1002/cc

their professional experience in business and industry. In addition, the use of adjunct faculty reduces costs, adds flexibility, and allows more agility to meet new educational market demands or niches. These are some of the tangible and intangible dimensions that competent and committed adjunct faculty members add to the value proposition at community colleges.

The literature on motivation, satisfaction, and educational quality could not adequately explain the experiences and successes that Rio Salado College has experienced with its adjunct faculty. An increasing number of studies confirm or reject these assumptions and attitudes about adjunct faculty satisfaction, commitment, and quality. The most applicable research has not only considered the relationship between the adjunct faculty and the local community college, but has examined this relationship in terms of the broader organizational, structural, and economic forces of the globalizing economy.

Slaughter and Leslie (1997) and Slaughter and Rhoades (2004) have expanded the view on faculty in the new economy by identifying the increasing use of adjunct faculty as a characteristic of an emerging academic capitalistic knowledge learning regime. The introduction of new technologies and the use of adjunct faculty become part of a strategy to increase efficiencies at community colleges. As faculty work is reconfigured, the use of adjunct faculty is expanded. Adjunct faculty in the community college provide greater institutional flexibility, cost savings, and greater managerial discretion that allow more market and market-like behaviors to increase entrepreneurial activities and generate new revenue streams (Slaughter and Rhoades, 2004).

Motivation and satisfaction take on new dimensions when adjunct faculty are examined in the light of the new economy and disaggregated from a single group, or groups, and as a workforce. For example, Wagoner (2004) has clearly shown that the satisfaction of adjunct faculty who are closely aligned to business and industry tends to be higher than in traditional academic disciplines.

Levin (2001) noted that the community college is increasingly integrated into the new, corporate, and globalizing economy, a process that has reshaped the nature of community colleges and their missions. Levin, Kater, and Wagoner (2006) have gone on to describe this transformation of community colleges and, by definition, the adjunct faculty workforce that comprises the majority of faculty labor. Within the cauldron of shrinking state funding, global competition, and disruptive technologies, the traditional comprehensive community college has transformed into a *nouveau* college described as "part transfer institution, economic development engine, social welfare agency, entrepreneurial institute, and baccalaureate and post-baccalaureate college" (Levin, Kater, and Wagoner, 2006, p. 134).

Adjunct faculty who work at a *nouveau* college will have differing characteristics in terms of motivation and satisfaction. Similarly, the questions surrounding educational quality must be reframed given the new technologies, new markets, and the new and globalizing context in which adjunct faculty work. Given this broader perspective on community colleges, how does an institution like Rio Salado College address and engage its adjunct faculty? What approaches have proven effective, and what is the impact on adjunct faculty? The best way to understand the Rio Salado systems approach is to start with an understanding of the culture and nature of the college itself.

An Astonishing Community College

Named after the Salt River, Rio Salado College is the largest of the ten Maricopa County Community Colleges in terms of head count. In 2006, Rio Salado had over forty-six thousand enrollments in credit courses and an additional fourteen thousand enrollments in noncredit programs (Bird, 2006). The size of Rio Salado results from over a decade of double-digit enrollment growth, an impressive feat for a college that was founded without walls in 1978. With growth as a source of funding, Rio Salado has shown a dynamic and consistent pattern of vitality.

When examining Rio Salado College's purposes, one can easily note the similarities between most community colleges' purpose statements, but with important differences. Rio Salado's community is a local and global community, reflecting the overall trend of globalization of the community college. The college is committed to serving local, national and international communities through e-learning and collaborative partnerships. It is through examining the organizational values, vision, and mission statements that the connection and similarities to new economy enterprises are most apparent. The stated college organizational values are customer focus, relentless improvement, inclusiveness, professionalism, and teamwork—all values that fit easily into a corporate setting in the new economy. The Rio Salado College Core Practices also communicate a market-like direction.

Rio Salado's vision statement is more ambitious when it states, "We astonish our customers" (Rio Salado, n.d., n.p.). This vision statement provides an insight into the culture. First, the use of the word *customer* denotes the awareness of a market where there is competition and choice. Second, *astonish* denotes an expectation to move beyond the notion of customer service that surpasses most business standards of satisfaction. Both meanings express the businesslike (Levin, Kater, and Wagoner, 2006) and marketlike (Slaughter and Rhoades, 2004) behaviors and language that reflect a clear comfort and ease with an entrepreneurial and business context of the new economy.

Rio Salado also has a lengthy history and experience with total quality management, organizational learning, continuous (and now relentless) improvement, and other processes that promote innovation and growth (Bird, 2006). These practices have been incorporated into how Rio Salado organizes and manages its internal processes. Rio Salado is the only educational organization in the state to earn the Arizona Governor's Quality Award as a result of on ongoing and deliberate culture of improvement (Bird, 2006). It was also a founding member of the Continuous Quality Improvement Network, a consortium of institutions, organizations, and businesses that examine quality practices to enhance the quality of education.

Leveraging digital technology has created new opportunities for Rio Salado. The college quickly moved to digital delivery of distance education as the Internet exploded in the 1990s. With this movement to e-learning, the traditional semester has been replaced with an ongoing, flexible college schedule that has twenty-six start dates; online courses start every two weeks. This will soon give way to daily start dates, enabling students to begin their courses at any time. In anticipation of growth and pressing production requirements, Rio Salado College has partnered with Dell and Microsoft to build its own learning management system, RioLearn, which is designed to accommodate over 100,000 online students.

Rio Salado College sees itself as a comprehensive community college—but comprehensive in a nontraditional way—a high-tech and innovative way. The college offers Sun Sounds of Arizona, a reading service for the visually disabled; KBAQ and KJZZ, the classical and National Public Radio stations for the Phoenix area; and a lifelong learning center. Levin, Kater, and Wagoner (2006) would describe Rio Salado as being a *nouveau* college because of its culture and overall orientation and awareness of markets and competition. Whatever the label or classification, Rio Salado College demonstrates a remarkable, and perhaps even an astonishing, integration into the new economy marked by its growth and status.

A Systems Approach with Adjunct Faculty

Rio Salado College was originally intended to be operated entirely through the use of adjunct faculty. The college recruited full-time, residential faculty, which now number twenty-eight, as the need or opportunity presented itself. The full-time faculty members serve as faculty chairs who oversee and manage the adjunct faculty according to their academic or occupational discipline.

As noted, Rio Salado's culture and organizational processes are unapologetically inspired by business and industry. Quickly approaching its thirtieth anniversary, Rio Salado College employs over 1,057 adjunct faculty to teach courses in a variety of formats. Currently, 550 adjunct faculty teach over 450 e-learning courses in general education, business, and relevant occupational courses. This represents a 52.2 percent increase in e-learning adjunct faculty and a 19.6 percent increase in adjunct faculty since 2003. Rio Salado has an extensive dual enrollment program where adjunct faculty members at local high schools teach college-level courses. Adjunct faculty also teach courses in adult basic education and workforce development (Bird, 2006). Finally, Rio Salado College pioneered and implemented a postbaccalaureate teacher preparation program in Arizona that provides teacher certification that is normally available only at a university.

Of the adjunct faculty who choose to teach at Rio Salado College, there is less than a 5 percent turnover, with 80 percent teaching for more than four semesters and 35 percent teaching for at least thirteen semesters. When adjunct faculty were surveyed and asked if they were actively seeking a full-time faculty position, 82 percent replied no. This indicates a stable adjunct faculty cohort with a majority not seeking employment, at least at the local community colleges.

The systems approach at Rio Salado College seeks to build an organizational infrastructure in order to accommodate adjunct faculty needs. The system, which comprises faculty chairs, adjunct faculty services, institutional advancement, library services, technology and instructional help desks, institutional research, course production and support, and instructional design services, supports and assists the adjunct faculty. Whole college support processes are aligned across disciplines, departments, and deans. The system takes care of operational needs so that the adjunct faculty can focus on their primary duty and passion: teaching. Rio Salado has intentionally designed a culture, strategies, and processes that address the specific needs of its adjunct faculty based on Maslow's hierarchy. The systems approach has developed organizational structures and supports to meet physiological and safety needs of adjunct faculty. Social and esteem needs of adjunct faculty are met by specific inclusion and collaboration strategies. Like its vision, Rio Salado has promoted strategies with high expectations for performance from adjunct faculty to help them fulfill self-actualization needs.

In addition, the infrastructure that supports students also supports adjunct faculty, who, in new economy parlance, are e-lancers (Malone, 2004). These adjunct faculty come with, or have to quickly acquire, advanced technology, digital communication, and project management skills. Adjunct faculty must be able to navigate the information superhighway. The systems approach aligns organizational resources toward adjunct faculty support while at the same time raising the quality and capacity to support students, especially online students. Of course, there will be individual variation from faculty member to faculty member—and from discipline to discipline. However, these strategies seem to address the real needs of the adjunct faculty as a group working at Rio Salado.

The Rio Salado college infrastructure has evolved from a systems approach to support adjunct faculty and students. It has simultaneously been designed to support full-time faculty as well. There are no overt status differences in the ability to acquire information, resources, or support, especially in terms of teaching roles. The full-time faculty member has the same course resources as the adjunct faculty member. Since full-time faculty will teach less than 1 percent of the courses, this makes sense. Rio Salado College uses a "one course, many sections" model in the design, development, production, and delivery of its online courses. The course content is exactly the same across all sections of a course, regardless of who is teaching the course section. The course content and materials are initially developed by the faculty chair or by an adjunct faculty developer, who then works closely with instructional design services and the faculty chair to develop content that meets the desired competencies and student learning outcomes. Instructional Design Services employs graphic artists, media specialists, editors, proofreaders, and designers. This design and development process creates an unbundling of the faculty role (Slaughter and Rhoades, 2004) that portions out critical tasks that would normally be performed by a full-time faculty member. The result is a single course that is highly standardized and designed for delivery by an adjunct or full-time faculty.

Systems for Support. Through this strategic systems approach, different college areas are integrated and involved in providing support to Rio Salado College's adjunct faculty. Each of these departments or areas provides specific services to ensure that real support is available. Like the over twenty-five thousand online students, the first contact with the college by an adjunct faculty may be through a Web page. Rio Salado's home page has a link to "Teach for Rio" that elicits eighty or more applications per week. The staffing for all courses is centralized through Faculty Services, often the first human contact made with the college. The managers of this department work in consultation with the faculty chairs to recruit and assign adjunct faculty to the more than three thousand sections offered each semester. Recruitment of adjunct faculty is an ongoing process throughout the year because e-learning course sections start every two weeks. In addition to the link on the college home page, Faculty Services recruits instructors by coordinating with Institutional Advancement's marketing specialists to place advertisements in local newspapers. Recruitment may also occur through organizational partners, social and professional networks of current faculty, and referrals from the community. All adjunct faculty candidates have their professional credentials reviewed by Faculty Services and the faculty chair. When a candidate has been interviewed and approved, personnel information and teaching preferences are recorded in the college's faculty information system (FIS) database. FIS assists Faculty Services in matching the course with the adjunct faculty's preferences. In contrast to many other community colleges, the adjunct faculty is not left alone to navigate through the semester after being handed the instructor's edition of the textbook. Once an adjunct faculty has taught a course, Faculty Services and Institutional Research provide feedback to the faculty chair who will review performance data, student and faculty evaluations, and teaching preferences in order to match the faculty with appropriate courses and modes of delivery.

Rio Salado's technology help desk supports students and adjunct faculty who teach online by troubleshooting technical, software, or connectivity problems. The technology help desk team is available around the clock. Adjunct faculty, students, and Rio Salado professional staff have access to the technology help desk in person, over the Internet, or on the telephone.

In harmony with the technology help desk, Rio Salado College has created an instructional help desk, designed specifically to assist e-learning adjunct faculty and students with content or course issues. Only experienced adjunct faculty who have been recommended by their faculty chair are qualified and recruited to staff the instructional help desk. This requirement not only provides knowledgeable support to students; it enables adjunct faculty to resolve issues with professional peers. The instructional help desk team provides new faculty orientation sessions, administrative assistance, consulting, and some technical assistance. This team also supports the faculty chair by acting as a liaison with the adjunct faculty. To track trends and promote improvement, a database is shared with the technology help desk. The instructional help desk also assists adjunct faculty in outreach and retention efforts through the Please Call program, where new online students are contacted during the first two weeks of class to ensure that they have successfully engaged the course work and overcome technical, time management, or other learning barriers. Tutoring services are available in person and by telephone, live chat, and e-mail. Additional tutoring is available through Smarthinking.com, an outsourced tutoring service.

Rio Salado's course production and support department publishes the digital content to RioLearn so that it is ready to be viewed online. This department also maintains the learning assessment databases and provides adjunct faculty with instructions, supplies, and discipline-specific materials. And although a "one course, many sections" model exists, the twenty-five hundred online sections may need some form of change or maintenance at any given time because of the twenty-six start dates during the year.

The college's library services were designed for both student and adjunct faculty populations. Adjunct faculty may request books, DVDs, or other materials from the library's collection by phone or online; these materials are then delivered to their homes. The library's Web site provides many resources for adjunct faculty, including online tutorials and writing labs. The library has an impressive collection of full-text electronic databases, including journal, magazine, and newspaper articles; images, encyclopedias; and e-books available through the Internet. A virtual library orientation is available to all adjunct faculty when they sign up to teach for the college. In addition, the college librarians provide reference services in person and by phone, e-mail, and an around-the-clock live chat service called Ask a Librarian.

Finally, the college's advisement and counseling service provides direct support to adjunct faculty. It offers personal and career counseling in-person, by phone, and by e-mail, offering a resource that adjunct faculty can easily refer to their students as the need arises.

Systems for Inclusion and Collaboration. The marginalization of adjunct faculty and their lack of integration into the community of scholars underlie the issue of educational quality. While there is an increased awareness, adjunct faculty are not always included in critical discussions with their peers. This is not for a lack of desire but because of time and other constraints. However, in the emerging new economic reality, the difficulty of involving part-time employees is commonplace in most workplaces, not just in higher education. This does not mean that inclusion and collaboration cannot be increased. The Rio Salado adjunct faculty motivation survey showed 61 percent of the adjunct faculty agree or strongly agree that ongoing deliberate attention is paid to including adjunct faculty in department-level discussions and decisions. This is a significant percentage given the issues surrounding the concerns over marginalization and claims of disintegration of adjunct faculty. At Rio Salado, the systems approach strategies for inclusion and collaboration include efforts by the faculty chairs and faculty developers.

Faculty Chairs. Adjunct faculty are organized into similar disciplines or departments. Generally one full-time residential faculty, designated as the faculty chair, oversees the discipline or department. Faculty chairs communicate with, mentor, and support the adjunct faculty in their disciplines. While the faculty chairs have been relieved by the support infrastructure of the more routine and mundane tasks, they still have duties in six areas: (1) teaching; (2) instructional leadership; (3) content and curriculum development, including data-driven improvements, textbook selection, and teaching and learning strategies; (4) department leadership, including supervising and evaluating adjunct faculty; (5) communication with students; and (6) participating on college and district committees, collegewide system projects or initiatives, and work as staff development trainers. Faculty chairs lead discipline dialogues, as well as department curriculum and assessment teams comprising adjunct faculty.

Faculty Developers. The faculty development coordinator, a designated full-time faculty member, directs the formal faculty development activities for adjunct faculty at Rio Salado College. Supporting the formal efforts are the faculty development committee, the faculty chairs, and the instructional helpdesk. These activities, which are well attended, include ongoing orientations for new faculty, biannual all-faculty learning experiences, effective online instruction workshops, and online professional development workshops. More workshops or seminars may be held within a department or discipline. At the district, there are in-person fall and spring professional development workshops offered by Rio Salado, the Maricopa Community Colleges, and the Maricopa Center for Learning and Instruction. The all-faculty learning experiences frequently highlight national speakers on current educational and business topics and trends. The adjunct faculty have the option to receive continuing education units for participating in many of these activities.

Each year the college recognizes an outstanding adjunct faculty from the various disciplines for teaching and contributions to assessment. The faculty chairs select the winners based on peer, student, and chair evaluations of their contribution to the discipline. The award-winning faculty members are honored in the presence of their peers at the all-faculty learning experience.

Because of the changing nature of technology, training is provided on how to teach online classes—moving beyond basic features to full mastery of all the technologies available to students. Adjunct faculty also have free tuition for up to six hours of courses at any of the Maricopa Community Colleges. Faculty Services also facilitates the application process for professional growth funds that are available through the Maricopa Community Colleges for conferences and workshops.

College-level communication with adjunct faculty occurs through the *Inside Rio* newsletter, the RioLearn Portal, and faculty development mailings. However, the primary communication is from the discipline faculty chair and includes mailings, e-mail, teleconferences, departmental SharePoint Portal Services, and in-person meetings. The human, physical, and financial resources adjunct faculty survey showed that 80 percent of respondents agreed or strongly agreed that their faculty chair shared with them the information they needed to do their job. These survey data were very favorable from the perspective of the adjunct faculty, indicating that 95 percent of adjunct faculty felt that their work helped Rio Salado accomplish its mission, 84 percent of respondents indicated that they felt respected on the job, and 80 percent indicated that they felt valued for the quality of the work they did. In terms of compensation and support, 84 percent agreed or strongly agreed that the workload for their position was fair, and 79 percent agreed or strongly agreed that they had access to the resources needed to do their job well.

Systems for Astonishment and High Expectations. The Rio Salado College culture is based on the principles and practices of relentless quality improvement with customer astonishment as an organizational aspiration. Astonishment occurs when the customers' future needs are anticipated or exceeded. The professional staff, faculty, and administration work together to analyze processes, improve them, and monitor the results. In 2002, faculty chairs developed college expectations for adjunct faculty with explicit performance standards and articulated at the discipline level in a department expectations statement. These statements clarified expected response times, requirements for grading and feedback, and other professional standards. They also emphasized how faculty, students, and the college systems work together to create effective teaching and learning. The involvement and input by the adjunct faculty was critical since they represent the college when they work with the students. Ultimately the adjunct faculty were entrusted with assessing what was realistic. Transparent expectations for the systems and the adjunct faculty contribute to greater communication and collaboration. Seventy-seven percent of the adjunct faculty agreed or strongly agreed that ongoing, deliberate attention is paid to agreement on consistently high expectations for distance learning instruction at Rio Salado College, as well as to meeting these expectations.

Because these expectation statements were developed by the adjunct faculty with their faculty chair, there is increased inclusion, buy-in, and perceived value by the adjunct faculty members, and a reality check on the rest of the system to know if the stated expectations are realistic to make astonishment possible.

Implications for Practice. The systems approach at Rio Salado College has built an organizational infrastructure to accommodate adjunct faculty needs within the context of a new and globalizing economy. The results are a stable, qualified, and proven cohort of over 1,057 adjunct faculty teaching courses who indicate that they feel a high level of support. The 2003 adjunct faculty motivation survey showed that 85 percent of respondents agreed or strongly agreed that the college pays ongoing, deliberate attention to providing support for its adjunct faculty. In additional comments in this survey, respondents praised the support services and activities that allow them to focus on quality teaching and learning at the college. Another 80 percent reported that they felt respected and valued for the quality of their work.

While the systems approach at Rio Salado College has been a demonstrable success, it still has its challenges. The sheer growth of student enrollments puts strains on the areas and departments in terms of communication, collaboration, and coordination of complex processes. At the same time, some adjunct faculty members have reverted to more traditional teaching practices. Finally, increased competition from other community colleges that are becoming more integrated into the new economy creates greater competition for student enrollments and for the highly skilled adjunct faculty who can teach using new technologies and professional skills.

The day of the adjunct faculty in community colleges is here—and will remain here for the foreseeable future. Understanding adjunct faculty behaviors will not only need to take into account the traditional issues of motivation and educational quality, but will need to do so within an increasingly complex and globalizing new economy.

References

Ashburn, E. "The Few, the Proud, the Professors." *Chronicle for Higher Education,* Oct. 6, 2006, p. A10.

Bird, L. "A Nontraditional Approach to Educating Tomorrow's Workforce." *Community College Journal,* 2006, 77(3), 48–51.

Cason, F., Estep, J., and Hixson, K. "Part-Timers Unite! Adjunct Professors Struggle for Equal Rights." *New Art Examiner,* 1999, 26(5), 38–42.

Clery, S. *Faculty in Academe.* Washington, D.C.: National Education Association, 1998.

Cohen, A. M., and Brawer, F. B. *The American Community College.* (4th ed.) San Francisco: Jossey-Bass, 2003.

Davis, H. M., Helminski, L., and Smith, V. C. "The Rio Salado College Systems Approach to Strategic Success with Adjunct Faculty." In D. Wallin (ed.), *Adjunct Faculty in Community Colleges: An Academic Administrator's Guide to Recruiting, Supporting, and Retaining Great Teachers.* Bolton, Mass.: Anker, 2005.

Gappa, J. M., and Leslie, D. W. *The Invisible Faculty: Improving the Status of Part-Timers in Higher Education.* San Francisco: Jossey-Bass, 1993.

Jacoby, D. "Effects of Part-Time Faculty Employment on Community College Graduation Rates." *Journal of Higher Education,* 2006, 77(6), 1081–1103.

Keim, M. C. "Two-Year College Faculty: A Research Update." *Community College Review,* 1989, 17(3), 34–43.

Levin, J. *Globalizing the Community College: Strategies for Change in the Twenty-First Century.* New York: Palgrave, 2001.

Levin, J., Kater, S., and Wagoner, R. *Community College Faculty: At Work in the New Economy.* New York: Palgrave, 2006.

Malone, T. W. *The Future of Work: How the New Order of Business Will Shape Your Organization, Your Management Style and Your Life.* Boston: Harvard Business School Press, 2004.

Rhoades, G. *Managed Professionals: Unionized Faculty and Restructuring Academic Labor.* Albany: State University of New York Press, 1998.

Rio Salado College. *Vision and Mission.* Tempe, Ariz.: Rio Salado College, n.d.

Roueche, J., Roueche, S., and Milliron, M. *Strangers in Their Own Land: Part-Time Faculty in American Community Colleges.* Washington, D.C.: Community College Press, 1995.

Slaughter, S., and Leslie, L. L. *Academic Capitalism: Politics, Policies, and the Entrepreneurial University.* Baltimore, Md.: Johns Hopkins University Press, 1997.

Slaughter, S., and Rhoades, G. *Academic Capitalism and the New Economy.* Baltimore, Md.: Johns Hopkins University Press, 2004.

Sonner, B. S. "A Is for Adjunct: Examining Grade Inflation in Higher Education." *Journal of Education for Business,* 2000, 76(1), 5–8.

U.S. Department of Education. *National Study of Postsecondary Faculty.* Washington, D.C.: U.S. Department of Education, 2003.

Wagoner, R. "The Contradictory Faculty: Part-Time Faculty at Community Colleges." Unpublished doctoral dissertation, University of Arizona, 2004.

VERNON C. SMITH is dean of institutional effectiveness at Rio Salado College in Tempe, Arizona.

8

As community colleges become dependent on a contingent workforce, the recruitment, retention, and motivation of quality part-time faculty become an institutional priority. This chapter presents an overview of the practices of three exemplary colleges in providing innovative professional development for part-time faculty.

Part-Time Faculty and Professional Development: Notes from the Field

Desna L. Wallin

While community colleges are almost uniformly aware of the important role adjunct faculty play, they vary widely in their approach to recruiting, retaining, motivating, and supporting adjunct faculty. This chapter highlights three colleges with programs that target part-time faculty and attempt to integrate them into the culture of the college. These colleges, and many others like them, are making significant efforts to support their adjunct faculty. They have demonstrated that quality professional development experiences can be designed and implemented even by colleges with limited resources.

Characteristics of Part-Time Faculty

However they are labeled, part-time faculty have become increasingly important to the success of community colleges. The 2004 National Study of Postsecondary Faculty reports that about 67 percent of faculty employed in public two-year institutions work part time (Cataldi, Fahimi, Bradburn, and Zimbler, 2005). Given the budget pressures of community colleges, it is likely that adjunct faculty will remain a permanent part of the community college instructional landscape.

Adjuncts are valued for their specialized knowledge and real-world experience, as well as their close connection to business and industry. They also bring obvious economic benefits to the college inasmuch as they are paid much less than full-time faculty and in most cases are not eligible for benefits. Often part-time faculty do not require office space or clerical support

NEW DIRECTIONS FOR COMMUNITY COLLEGES, no. 140, Winter 2007 © 2007 Wiley Periodicals, Inc.
Published online in Wiley InterScience (www.interscience.wiley.com) • DOI: 10.1002/cc.306

(Witt, Wattenbarger, Gollattscheck, and Suppiger, 1994). Moreover, they provide the college with a certain amount of flexibility. Although they may not have the credentials or the teaching experience of full-time faculty, many adjunct faculty bring a fresh and reality-based perspective to the classroom. They are perceived as credible by students who appreciate up-to-date perspectives. Without a doubt, part-time faculty add diversity, enrichment, and scheduling flexibility to the institution.

Contrary to conventional wisdom, most studies have shown that part-time faculty members are as effective as full-time faculty in terms of meeting student outcomes. Students learn as much, perform as well, and are as likely to be retained when taught by part-time faculty as when taught by full-time faculty. Adjunct faculty have no more discipline problems than full-time faculty, and their student evaluations are comparable to those of full-time faculty (Leslie and Gappa, 2002).

Adjunct faculty members, like the majority of their students, are adult learners who bring a variety of backgrounds and experiences to the classroom. They tend to be problem-centered learners rather than subject-centered learners and are more likely to be motivated by internal factors than external factors. They want to believe that they are adding value to their students' lives (Wallin, 2005).

Nevertheless, it is accurate to assume that adjunct faculty may not be as involved or as knowledgeable about student services, financial aid, health services, and library services as their full-time colleagues. Thus, it is imperative that administrators be sensitive to the needs of adjunct faculty and be sure they have access to the same information and resources as full-time faculty. Such information is particularly important if the part-time faculty teach in the evening, on weekends, or at off-campus sites where the full complement of services may not be available. It is the responsibility of management to recruit, evaluate, and retain successful part-time faculty. One way to support them is to provide a strong professional development program tailored to their specific needs. These faculty need to understand what the institution expects of them through thorough orientation programs and ongoing support. Realizing that part-time faculty choose to teach for a variety of reasons, administrators need to be cognizant of the best ways to integrate them into the culture of the institution. Roueche, Roueche, and Milliron (1995) emphasize the importance of integrating part-time faculty and recognizing them as "important players in the teaching and learning process in the interest of providing quality instruction . . . and ultimately in the interest of establishing and maintaining the college's reputation for teaching excellence" (p. 120).

Examples of Exemplary Support

The three colleges highlighted in this chapter represent the diversity inherent in American community colleges. One is a relatively small college in a rural area of Texas, one is a medium-sized college in an industrial and agricultural region in Illinois, and the third is a large college in an urban environment in Washington State. Adjuncts comprise nearly two-thirds of the faculty at each college. Moreover, these colleges struggle to balance the professional development needs of full- and part-time faculty. The colleges do not have large budgets or foundation support for their initiatives. Rather, the senior leadership at each college recognizes the vital role adjuncts play in meeting the needs of students and fulfilling the historic community college mission of access, affordability, and equity. Through the commitment and creativity of leaders, each of the colleges has crafted innovative and effective initiatives to meet the needs of adjunct faculty at each institution.

Northeast Texas Community College. The Northeast Texas Community College campus is situated on a 220-acre farmstead in the middle of rolling hills. The college has found its rural location to be both a benefit and a challenge. One of the challenges is having a sufficient critical mass of part-time faculty available at any one time for training and professional development. To address this important issue, the college partnered with neighboring Paris Junior College, Collin County Community College District, Tyler Junior College, and Tomball College to develop the Academy for Part-Time Teachers, designed to help acclimate new part-time faculty to the community college teaching environment. It uses online delivery as the primary tool for discussion and learning. An advisory committee of representatives from the partnering colleges, the business sector, and a statewide leadership and professional development consortium provides input and takes an active role in establishing goals and evaluating the overall effectiveness of the academy.

The purpose of the academy is to help faculty develop skills in designing and providing instruction that is consistent with the colleges' commitment to excellence. To meet these goals, the academy provides twenty-four hours of training through a combination of live and online delivery. The components of the training include an orientation, in-service workshops, independent study, online discussions using Web-based course software, teacher partnering, classroom observations, and a summative symposium. The online teaching modules are reinforced by classroom observations, linkages with teaching partners, and a final capstone: a self-reflection paper summarizing the academy experience.

To ensure that all part-time faculty can benefit from the training, each participant receives instruction regarding the access and use of the course software. Four training modules are presented over a four-week period. All participants are expected to log in several times each week, complete the required assignments, and engage in dialogue with other part-time teaching colleagues. The teaching modules contain reading material and discussion questions. The topics for the teaching modules are intended to introduce the new part-time faculty to the environment and history of the community college as well as provide specific assistance in teaching techniques and classroom management. The modules discuss teaching in today's community colleges, planning for effective undergraduate teaching and learning, helping students become successful learners, teaching adult learners in the community college environment, teaching with technology, effective questioning, and assessment techniques. A series of questions for discussion and related links follows each module.

The evaluation model of the academy includes the assessment of the individual participant's reactions and performance, as well as an attempt to determine the impact on student learning. For example, a recent annual assessment determined that courses taught by part-time faculty who graduated from the academy (by completing all the required assignments and workshops) received higher ratings from students than those not taught by academy graduates. On the evaluation item "instructor encourages students," 65 percent of the academy graduates were rated higher than instructors who did not complete the academy. Similarly, 59 percent of graduates were rated higher on "instructor uses class time well" and "instructor explains concepts well." Finally, 47 percent were rated higher for "instructor is prepared for teaching," and 41 percent were rated higher for "instructor has a fair grading system."

The Academy for Part-Time Teachers is based on the philosophy that part-time teachers are a major asset of the college, can improve their teaching, and need support and encouragement. When reflecting on this program, several participants discussed the benefits of the program. One noted that she uses "one of the ideas from the sessions for every class I teach." Another commented, "Attending the academy has given me a greater sense of security in the classroom."

Black Hawk College. Black Hawk College, located on the Mississippi River in Moline, Illinois, is a medium-sized college in an agricultural and industrial area. The part-time faculty are unionized and have recently negotiated a five-year agreement covering wages, hours, and working conditions.

The Center for Teaching and Learning at Black Hawk provides full- and part-time faculty support services for teaching and online learning. The college has found that offering specific activities geared to part-time faculty and creating collegial relationships among faculty has increased the stability of the part-time workforce. Of particular note is the Adjunct Academy Connect with the Best . . . You Deserve It, an annual adjunct faculty teaching enrichment event. This all-day event features a unique partnership between two community colleges: Black Hawk College and Scott Community College in Davenport, Iowa. The sessions are not mandatory, and faculty are not paid to attend. However, adjunct faculty members who lead panel discussions or roundtable sessions are paid a small honorarium.

The day begins with a continental breakfast and roundtable best practice sessions led by fellow adjuncts. The lunch includes "birds of a feather" sessions in which faculty who teach similar content are brought together to discuss issues of importance in their respective disciplines. The early afternoon features a keynote speaker on a topic of relevance to adjunct faculty. For example, one recent keynote speaker highlighted contemporary community college students with emphasis on generational differences and the challenges of teaching across generations. Most recently, the keynote speaker dealt with the impact of socioeconomic diversity on student success and the values that students bring to the classroom. Following the keynote speaker, the group breaks into discussion workshops to discuss the practical applications of the content of the keynote presentation and to get involved in more in-depth teaching topics.

The Adjunct Academy has created a stronger network among adjunct faculty from both sides of the river and has encouraged sharing of resources and collaboration that extends beyond the classroom. Administrators at both institutions emphasize their appreciation for the adjunct faculty's academic qualifications, teaching expertise, and experience in the field. They promote the academy as professional development specifically targeting the expressed needs of part-time faculty. The event is linked to teaching, encourages networking, and provides a variety of opportunities to share strategies for improving student learning. Most important, evaluations have shown that adjunct faculty members believe they are valued and appreciated by the college.

Tacoma Community College. Tacoma Community College is an urban college serving a diverse population. Understanding the importance of their large cadre of part-time faculty, Tacoma Community College, with the support of the president and strategic guidance and leadership from the professional development coordinator, developed the Adjunct Faculty Institute. Admission to the institute is competitive: only twenty adjunct faculty are accepted for a ten-week learning experience. To be eligible, faculty must be part time and be scheduled to teach a class during the term of the institute. The applicants must write a letter that describes their teaching experience, learning expectations, and career goals. The letter, along with a résumé, is submitted to a team of instructional administrators who select the participants. The participants receive a stipend of five hundred dollars on successful completion of the institute.

The institute meets weekly for a two-hour period in the late afternoon. Participants are given a text on college teaching with reading assignments for most weeks, periodic writing assignments, and some Internet research. The main topic each week is planned with specific time for presentation of new ideas, problem solving, and discussion. As part of the learning experience, different permutations of small group work and assessment techniques are modeled in the presentations. Topics for discussion include developing a philosophy of learning and teaching, student motivation, adult learning theory, instructional design, collaborative learning, assessment of student learning, dealing with challenging students, and academic honesty.

The college has found that adjunct faculty members who participate in the institute are more likely to stay with the college, thus addressing ongoing recruitment and retention issues. While the college has not conducted empirical research to determine if there is increased effectiveness of faculty who have completed the institute, the anecdotal evidence is positive.

While the Adjunct Faculty Institute is competitive and limited to twenty participants, the college supports its adjunct faculty in a variety of other ways, including orientation, financial support for conferences, access to all full-time faculty professional development activities, and membership on the faculty professional development committee. Of special note is the annual adjunct faculty gathering, an evening dinner for all adjuncts, with updates on college activities, small group meetings with deans and department chairs, and an opportunity to ask questions prior to the start of the term. The president and other senior administrators attend and participate as well. Faculty who attend the adjunct faculty gathering are compensated for their participation, a recognition of the importance of their time and commitment to the college and their students.

Tacoma Community College adjunct support has as its goals to enhance knowledge, skills, and attitudes in college learning and teaching. The institute and other activities support the college's desire to develop its faculty, encourage adjunct faculty to remain at the college, and enhance faculty opportunities for continued contracts and full-time positions. Active part-time faculty support is a three-way win: for the college, for the faculty, and for the students.

What Every Community College Can Do

While colleges vary greatly in the resources they expend for both salaries and professional development, there are things that all colleges can do. Bradley (2007) summarized the American Association of University Professors' recommendations, many of which are as appropriate for community college adjuncts as they are for university part-time faculty. Twelve recommendations directly applicable to adjunct faculty in community colleges follow:

- Be sure that the terms and conditions of every appointment are stated in writing.
- Provide every faculty member with a telephone number, even if it is the general office number, and an institutional e-mail account.
- Create dedicated space for adjunct faculty to have access to computers, photocopying, file storage, and a place to meet with students.
- Consider alternative or tiered pay scales for faculty who have taught long term as adjuncts.
- Provide funding for conferences.
- Invite adjunct faculty to faculty meetings, and provide adjuncts with faculty meeting minutes.
- Prepare a handbook for new part-time faculty that provides the basics of departmental functions, forms, student services, grading scales and procedures, academic honesty policies, sample syllabi, and safety and security procedures.
- Establish systems of communication between supervisors and part-time faculty.

NEW DIRECTIONS FOR COMMUNITY COLLEGES • DOI: 10.1002/cc

- Provide accessible professional development opportunities.
- Create a mentoring system to help integrate adjunct faculty in the college culture.
- Provide part-time faculty with access to library, recreational, and parking facilities.
- Treat adjunct faculty as valued colleagues and encourage inclusiveness and collegiality.

Conclusion

The twelve recommendations embody meaningful actions that can be taken, without great expense, to support the critical work of adjunct faculty in community colleges. Many colleges, as illustrated by the three innovative colleges highlighted in this chapter, are putting forth outstanding effort to support and reward the work of their adjunct colleagues. Yet much more needs to be done. While community colleges are known as teaching institutions and their full-time faculty are committed to helping students, they cannot do it alone. It is only through the work of adjunct faculty meeting the need for specialized courses, high-enrollment courses, and clinical and laboratory assistance that community colleges are able to accomplish their mission of accessibility, equity, and affordability for the thousands of students aspiring to better their life circumstances through America's community colleges.

References

Bradley, G. "How to Help Adjuncts." *Inside Higher Ed,* Mar. 13, 2007, n.p.

Cataldi, E. F., Fahimi, M., Bradburn, E. M., and Zimbler, L. *2004 National Study of Post-Secondary Faculty Report on Faculty and Instructional Staff.* Washington, D.C.: U.S. Department of Education, 2005.

Leslie, D. W., and Gappa, J. M. "Part-Time Faculty: Competent and Committed." In C. L. Outcalt (ed.), *Community College Faculty: Characteristics, Practices, and Challenges.* New Directions for Community College, no. 118, San Francisco: Jossey-Bass, 2002.

Roueche, J., Roueche, S., and Milliron, M. *Strangers in Their Own Land: Part-Time Faculty in American Community Colleges.* Washington, D.C.: Community College Press, 1995.

Wallin, D. L. (ed.). *Adjunct Faculty in Community Colleges: An Academic Administrator's Guide to Recruiting, Supporting, and Retaining Great Teachers.* Bolton, Mass.: Anker, 2005.

Witt, A., Wattenbarger, J., Gollattscheck, J., and Suppiger, J. *America's Community Colleges.* Washington, D.C.: Community College Press, 1994.

DESNA L. WALLIN *is an associate professor in the department of Lifelong Education, Administration, and Policy at the University of Georgia.*

9

This chapter explores community college faculty satisfaction related to four specific variables.

Part-Time Faculty Satisfaction Across Missions and Disciplines

Richard L. Wagoner

As Valadez and Anthony (2001) point out, there is a paucity of studies of part-time faculty satisfaction in community colleges. Until their study, only anecdotal accounts of satisfaction were available in the scholarly literature. Analyzing data from the 1993 National Survey of Postsecondary Faculty (NSOPF 93), Valadez and Anthony found mixed results regarding the satisfaction and commitment of community college part-time faculty. With regard to the demands and rewards, they found no difference between the satisfaction of part-time faculty at two-year colleges and part-time faculty at four-year institutions. Like Gappa and Leslie (1997), Valadez and Anthony aggregate two-year, part-time faculty as a single group.

Up to this point, the literature on part-time faculty has presented a confusing, or at least heterogeneous, picture. Depending on how one chooses to study the question, part-timers might appear to be satisfied with their work (Gappa and Leslie, 1997; Valadez and Anthony, 2001), exploited (Dubson, 2001), or somewhere in the middle (Roueche, Roueche, and Milliron, 1995). For many, this presents a conundrum (Gappa and Leslie, 1997) with no clear solution. For others, it calls for clearer and more just policies and procedures. I believe that viewing the use of part-time faculty through the lens of the new economy and the changes in labor it has brought over the past thirty years provides a method of understanding the heterogeneous nature of part-timers in community colleges.

NEW DIRECTIONS FOR COMMUNITY COLLEGES, no. 140, Winter 2007 © 2007 Wiley Periodicals, Inc.
Published online in Wiley InterScience (www.interscience.wiley.com) • DOI: 10.1002/cc307

Methods

This chapter provides a quantitative analysis of community college faculty satisfaction data using the 1999 National Studies of Postsecondary Faculty (NSOPF 99). As discussed in Chapter Three, there are two important bifurcations of community college faculty when one conceives of them as a form of new economy labor. By focusing on the differences between part-timers and among full-timers and part-timers from both the arts and sciences and the vocational and training groups, this chapter's analysis illuminates differences that may not be evident when looking at faculty in the aggregate. Therefore, the chapter is concerned exclusively with the responses of both full-time and part-time faculty in community colleges, comparing them to each other as well as by the two-group disaggregation discussed in Chapter Three. That desegregation combines the work of Levin, Kater, and Wagoner (2006) and Benjamin (1998) into two groups: (1) arts and sciences and (2) vocational and training.

The five variables considered in the study are satisfaction with the job overall, satisfaction with job security, satisfaction with advancement opportunities, satisfaction with salary, and satisfaction with benefits. Taken from the area of demands and rewards (Valadez and Antony, 2001), these variables serve to indicate the relative desirability of part-time positions in the faculty labor market. Faculty responded to each of these questions with answers varying from 1 to 4, with 1 = very dissatisfied, 2 = somewhat dissatisfied, 3 = somewhat satisfied, and 4 = very satisfied. In addition to these satisfaction variables, I include analysis of faculty response to the statement, "If I had it to do over again, I would still choose an academic career." For this variable, the possible responses were as follows: 1 = strongly disagree, 2 = disagree, 3 = agree, and 4 = strongly agree. This variable functions to gauge how dedicated faculty members are to the academic life, regardless of their satisfaction with the demands and rewards of their positions.

As a baseline, I compare the aggregate mean responses for each variable for all part-time and full-time faculty. From there, I compare the means of responses to each variable for full- as well as part-time faculty from the arts and sciences group and from the vocational and training group. After these initial comparisons of means, I discuss results from weighted least square regressions that control for gender, age, number of years at the institution (seniority), number of classes taught at the institution, highest degree attained, and race.

Findings

Aggregate mean results for each of the four demand and rewards variables show that full-time faculty are more satisfied than part-time faculty in terms of job security, advancement opportunities, salary, and benefits. Full-time faculty mean responses are 3.34 for security compared to 2.73 for part-timers. In this variable, all part-timers are less than somewhat satisfied with their security, and full-timers are more than somewhat satisfied. All faculty are less than somewhat satisfied with their advancement opportunities and salary, with a mean response for full-timers of 2.93 and 2.71, respectively, and 2.45 and 2.56 for part-time faculty. Of all the demand and reward variables, part-timers are the least satisfied with their benefits (2.30), while their full-time counterparts are more than somewhat satisfied (3.13). Even in the aggregate, it is clear that part-time faculty are less satisfied than full-timers regarding the demands and rewards of their positions. Based on these results, part-time faculty are less than somewhat satisfied in each area. In addition, one might argue that with part-time faculty less than somewhat satisfied with each of these variables and full-timers less than somewhat satisfied with two of them, community colleges need to better address how they meet faculty expectations in these four areas.

When college faculty are disaggregated, a more nuanced picture emerges—one that reinforces the conceptualization of faculty that undergirds the new economy model. In each of the four categories, part-time faculty from the arts and sciences group are less satisfied than those from the vocational and training group. In other words, the aggregate mean responses for part-time faculty serve as a dividing line for the gap between the two groups in each case. Remarkably, arts and sciences part-timers indicate being closer to feeling somewhat dissatisfied in all but the job security variable, with mean responses below 2.50 regarding advancement opportunities (2.32), salary (2.41), and benefits (2.14). Vocational and training part-timers do not drop below a mean of 2.50 for any of the variables. While one might believe these results simply show that arts and sciences faculty members are less satisfied, the averages for full-time faculty do not support such a hypothesis. In fact, they indicate exactly the opposite: full-time faculty members of the arts and sciences group are more satisfied than those from the vocational and training group in each of the four variables, so there would appear to be no connection to satisfaction due simply to one's academic discipline. Of all these variables, satisfaction is perhaps the most telling, as part-time vocational and training faculty have the highest mean of all of the four groups, at 2.76. While this still indicates that they are less than somewhat satisfied, vocational part-timers are the most satisfied with their salaries at colleges, which might be best supported by the fact that of the four groups, they are the least dependent on these salaries.

Results from the overall satisfaction variable illustrate the same pattern as those for demands and rewards. Part-time arts and sciences faculty are less satisfied overall (3.15) than vocational and training part-time faculty (3.39), a relationship that is reversed for full-time faculty, where arts and sciences members are slightly more satisfied (3.33) than those from the vocational group (3.29). As with the salary variable, part-time vocational and training faculty are more satisfied overall than any of the other groups, with arts and sciences part-timers being the least satisfied. This result clearly illuminates a significant rift in the perceptions and experiences of these two part-time groups, one that is not mirrored in their full-time counterparts, who show similar responses.

As the demand and reward and overall satisfaction responses indicate, part-time faculty from the arts and sciences group are less satisfied than those from the vocational and training group. This situation is reversed for the full-time groups, serving to intensify satisfaction differences between part-timers and full-timers in the arts and sciences, while ameliorating differences found between vocational and training part- and full-time faculty. It is significant to note, then, that in response to whether they would choose an academic career again, arts and sciences part-timers are more likely to do so (3.23) than are vocational and training part-timers (3.16). For this variable, vocational and training faculty have the lowest mean. The full-time faculty groups remain consistent for this variable, with arts and sciences faculty more willing to pursue an academic life (3.49) than the vocational and training group (3.34). These results delineate the divisions both between part-time and full-time faculty and among part-time faculty groups, a division that supports the conceptualization of part-time faculty described in Chapter Three.

After analyzing the aggregate and group mean responses discussed above, I conducted weighted least squares regressions for each of the six variables, comparing differences between the disaggregated groups while controlling for gender, age, number of years at the institution (seniority), number of classes taught at the institution, highest degree attained, and race. Because space does not allow for a complete reporting of those results here, I highlight the most relevant findings. Most important, the regressions indicated that the findings from the means analysis are robust. The regression analysis also indicated important differences that result from one's level of education and gender.

As with the simple means tests, part-time faculty from the vocational and training group were significantly more satisfied in each of the four demand and reward categories: job security ($t < .05$), advancement opportunities ($t < .001$), salary ($t < .001$), and benefits ($t < .001$). Amplifying these results, faculty members who had earned a doctorate were significantly less satisfied in each of the variables. As the doctorate is much more likely to be held by faculty in the arts and sciences group, controlling for this variable had the potential to eliminate the statistical significance of the lower satisfaction of arts and sciences part-timers, but it did not. In addition, men were more satisfied than women for each of the four variables. This is important, as men are much more likely to be members of the vocational and training group than women, while men and women have virtually identical representation in the arts and sciences part-time group. As with the variable for highest degree attained, a variable that might have eliminated the significance of the differences between these groups did not, indicating that the satisfaction differences between the groups are robust.

Regression results for the full-time groups were somewhat different but also support the conceptualization of faculty as new economy labor. Importantly, there was no statistically significant difference between the two full-time groups regarding their satisfaction with job security and salary. The two significant differences ($t < .05$), satisfaction with advancement opportunities and benefits, indicate that vocational faculty are less satisfied than their arts and sciences counterparts, a reversal of the trend in the part-time data. Highest degree attained provided interesting results for full-time faculty as well. Faculty members who have attained a first professional degree were significantly less satisfied in each of the four categories, particularly regarding security ($t < .01$) and benefits ($t < .001$). In both cases, the coefficient is less than negative four-tenths, making the finding important in terms of the size of the difference as well as significant statistically. The coefficients for faculty members with first professional degrees are also fairly large for satisfaction with advancement opportunities ($-.303$) and salary ($-.304$); in both cases, the significance exists at a more marginal level ($t < .1$), however. Taken together, these results suggest that a faculty member who is more likely to have connections to the nonacademic sector and would possess skills that would be sought by private corporations, that is, a faculty member who has attained a first professional degree, is significantly more likely to be dissatisfied with the demands and rewards of a full-time faculty position, a distinct difference from the results from the part-time faculty.

Part-time faculty from the vocational and training group were also significantly more satisfied with their positions overall ($t < .001$) than were their counterparts in the arts and sciences. As with the demand and rewards variables, faculty members who have attained a doctorate degree are significantly less satisfied overall with their positions ($t < .001$), reinforcing the interpretation that those who are most immersed in traditional academic practices are more likely to be dissatisfied with a part-time position. There is no statistically significant difference between members of the two full-time faculty groups with their positions overall. Once again, however, full-time faculty members who have attained a first professional degree are less satisfied with their positions overall ($t < .001$). Beyond its statistical significance, this result is also the largest in terms of its coefficient ($-.753$); this difference of three-quarters of a point in satisfaction reinforces the findings from the demands and rewards variables, indicating that those who are best trained to profit in the private sector have the most reservations about their full-time academic positions.

The data concerning whether a faculty member would choose an academic career again support the conceptualization of community college faculty as new economy labor. By themselves, the means between the two part-time groups are statistically significant, indicating that part-time faculty from the vocational and training group would be less likely to choose an academic career again. While the coefficient ($-.073$) for this difference is minimal and its statistical significance is eliminated after controlling for the included independent variables, it must be regarded as important considering that vocational part-timers were significantly more satisfied overall and in all of the demand and reward variables. Full-time faculty from the vocational group are less satisfied ($t < .05$), but the amount of difference is quite small—less than one-tenth of a point. This suggests that the finding may not be important, regardless of its statistical significance, supporting the satisfaction findings that full-time faculty members of the two groups tend not to demonstrate statistically significant or important differences.

Discussion

Clearly the results of this study demonstrate significant and important differences both between part-time and full-time faculty and among part-time faculty groups in community colleges regarding satisfaction with the demands and rewards of their positions, their overall satisfaction, and their desire to choose an academic career again. While no scholar has ever argued that there are not differences between full-time and part-time faculty satisfaction, it has been suggested that these differences are hard to categorize because of the heterogeneity of part-timers and their motivations (Gappa and Leslie, 1993, 1997; Rouche, Rouche, and Milliron, 1995). The general means comparisons from the beginning of the chapter indicate that even in broad terms, there are discernable differences with regard to the group to which a faculty member belongs and that those groups are clearly tied to two of the competing missions of community colleges, which can be understood in terms of their relationship to the private, for-profit business sector.

Succinctly stated, part-time faculty members who have been trained and teach in a traditional academic discipline are significantly less satisfied with positions at a community college than are full-time faculty and those part-timers who have closer ties to the private sector, which allows them to market themselves to multiple employers and profit from their skills and abilities. Conversely, full-time faculty members who have attained terminal professional degrees, qualifying them to profit in the private sector, are less satisfied with their academic positions when compared to other full-timers. These results are robust: the trends that are indicated in a simple comparison of means remain significant even after controlling for variables that have been identified as affecting satisfaction.

I believe the results from this analysis offer compelling evidence that the heterogeneity and motivations of part-timers can be better understood when one employs the conceptualization of community college faculty as a form of new economy labor. Most telling here is the gulf between part-timers in the arts and sciences and those in the vocational and training areas, particularly the fact that the simple explanation that full-time members of the arts and sciences might also be less satisfied than full-time members of the vocations does not hold. Part-time members of the vocational and training groups are able to use the individualization (Castells, 2000) of work to their advantage. In the new economy, part-time members of the vocational and training group possess skills that are valued in community colleges and in the private sector. These faculty members have the flexibility to exploit these skills to their fullest advantage in both colleges and the private sector. Arts and sciences part-timers, in contrast, do not possess skills that are highly valued outside academe and are unable to exploit these skills to their fullest potential without a full-time position in a college. This same logic also explains the differences in satisfaction between full-timers. Members of the arts and sciences have attained degrees and possess skills that are best capitalized on in colleges; therefore, they are quite satisfied with their positions. Full-time faculty members in the vocational and training disciplines, particularly those who have attained a professional degree, do possess skills that are valued in the private sector, but because of their full-time commitments to their college teaching, they are unable to capitalize on those skills.

References

Benjamin, E. "Variations in the Characteristics of Part-Time Faculty by General Fields of Instruction and Research." In D. W. Leslie (ed.), *The Growing Use of Part-Time Faculty: Understanding Causes and Effects*. New Directions for Higher Education, no. 104. San Francisco: Jossey-Bass, 1998.

Castells, M. *The Rise of the Network Society*. (2nd ed.) Malden, Mass.: Blackwell, 2000.

Dubson, M. (ed.). *Ghosts in the Classroom: Stories of Adjunct Faculty—and the Price We All Pay*. Boston: Camel's Back Books, 2001.

Gappa, J. M., and Leslie, D. W. *The Invisible Faculty: Improving the Status of Part-Timers in Higher Education*. San Francisco: Jossey-Bass, 1993.

Gappa, J. M., and Leslie, D. W. *Two Faculties or One? The Conundrum of Part-Timers in a Bifurcated Work Force*. Washington, D.C.: American Association for Higher Education, 1997.

Levin, J. S., Kater, S., and Wagoner, R. L. *Community College Faculty: At Work in the New Economy*. New York: Palgrave, 2006.

Roueche, J. E., Roueche, S. D., and Milliron, M. D. *Strangers in Their Own Land: Part-Time Faculty in American Community Colleges*. Washington, D.C.: Community College Press, 1995.

Valadez, J. R., and Anthony, J. S. "Job Satisfaction and Commitment of Two-Year College Part-Time Faculty." *Community College Journal of Research and Practice*, 2001, 25, 97–108.

RICHARD L. WAGONER *is assistant professor of higher education and organizational change in the Graduate School of Education and Information Studies at the University of California, Los Angeles.*

10

*This chapter summarizes resources from the recent litera-
ture on part-time community college faculty.*

Sources and Information: Community Colleges and Part-Time Faculty

Amy Liu

Part-time faculty comprise the majority of all faculty appointments at community colleges: 66.7 percent as of 2003 (Cataldi, Fahimi, Bradburn, and
Zimbler, 2005). As the previous chapters in this volume attest, part-time faculty members are an important community college constituent. The instruction and guidance they provide to students pursuing higher education
warrant due consideration and better understanding of their role as educators and their prominence within community colleges. This chapter provides additional information and an overview of recent scholarship related
to part-time faculty at community colleges. Taken together, this material
serves as useful resources for continued research in this area.

ERIC documents (references with "ED" numbers) may be read on
microfiche at approximately nine hundred libraries worldwide. In addition,
the full text of many documents is available online at http://www.eric.ed.gov.
Journal articles may be acquired through regular library channels, from the
originating journal publisher, or for a fee from the following article repro-
duction vendor: PP Ingenta; e-mail: ushelp@ingenta.com; phone: 617-395-
4046; toll-free: 1-800-296-2221; URL: http://www.ingenta.com/.

Who Are Part-Time Faculty?

Contrary to popular characterizations, part-time faculty are not simply
vagabond workers for hire without any institutional ties or greater responsibility to the comprehensive educational mission of the community college.

NEW DIRECTIONS FOR COMMUNITY COLLEGES, no. 140, Winter 2007 © 2007 Wiley Periodicals, Inc.
Published online in Wiley InterScience (www.interscience.wiley.com) • DOI: 10.1002/cc.308

As the following publications suggest, the picture is more complex; part-time faculty are not so dissimilar from their full-time counterparts. Moreover, how colleges integrate their part-time faculty is critical to their effectiveness as educators.

Leslie, D. W., and Gappa, J. M. "Part-Time Faculty: Competent and Committed." In C. L. Outcalt (ed.), *Community College Faculty: Characteristics, Practices, and Challenges.* New Directions for Community College, no. 118, San Francisco: Jossey-Bass, 2002. This chapter summarizes findings from an analysis of responses to a national survey of two thousand community college faculty members at 114 institutions conducted by the Council for the Study of Community Colleges. Using corroborating data from the 1992–1993 National Study of Postsecondary Faculty, Leslie and Gappa present and compare descriptions of part-time faculty in four categories: demographics, work profile, attitudes and motives, and opinions about teaching and learning. Their analysis indicates that these traits of part-time community college faculty resemble those of their full-time colleagues.

Banachowski, G. *Perspectives and Perceptions: A Review of the Literature on the Use of Part-Time Faculty in Community Colleges.* Toledo, Ohio: University of Toledo, 1996. (ED 398943). This literature review of ERIC publications since the late 1980s addresses the growth of part-time faculty in community colleges as well as the advantages and disadvantages of using part-time faculty for instruction delivery. Advantages to employing part-time faculty include resource conservation, institutional flexibility toward changing enrollment demands, industry experience, and individual teaching benefits for part-timers. Disadvantages cited include decreased full-time positions and supplemental pay for course overloads, role ambiguity, vulnerability to exploitation, and undermining of the teaching profession.

Valadez, J. R., and Anthony, J. S. "Job Satisfaction and Commitment of Two-Year College Part-Time Faculty." *Community College Journal of Research and Practice,* 2001, 25(2), 97–108. Using data drawn from the 1992–1993 National Study of Postsecondary Faculty, the authors use exploratory factor analysis to construct a multidimensional description of job satisfaction. The dimensions they measure are satisfaction with autonomy, satisfaction with students, satisfaction with demands and rewards, and overall job satisfaction. Comparative findings between two-year and four-year part-time faculty suggest that two-year college faculty members are less satisfied with their level of autonomy and with students, but equally concerned with matters of salary, benefits, and job security. For the most part, findings indicate that part-time faculty members are satisfied with their roles and their decisions to pursue academic careers. Nevertheless, the authors suggest that community colleges must develop a deeper understanding of job satisfaction and promote strategies that will continue improving the working conditions, job satisfaction, and commitment of part-time faculty members.

Jacoby, D. "Part-Time Community College Faculty and the Desire for Full-Time Tenure Track Positions: Results of a Single Institution Case Study." *Community College Journal of Research and Practice,* 2005, 29(2), 136–152. Contrary to the Valadez and Anthony (2001) study, Jacoby indicates that a majority of part-time faculty are not satisfied with the terms of their employment, particularly regarding their employment security. Using data from a single community college, the author employs logistic regression and finds that a major portion of part-time faculty both want and seek full-time teaching work. However, outside sources of income, age, and alternative sources of employment change the odds that a part-time person will desire full-time work. It is also important to note that the measures of satisfaction in this research are distinct from those reported by Valadez and Anthony, which do not directly address the desire for full-time employment. The findings in this study also refute some of the conclusions in the Leslie and Gappa (2002) study.

Wyles, B. A. "Adjunct Faculty in the Community Colleges: Realities and Challenges." In D. W. Leslie (ed.), *The Growing Use of Part-Time Faculty: Understanding Causes and Effects.* New Directions for Higher Education, no. 104. San Francisco: Jossey-Bass, 1998. Wyles states that the central concern regarding part-time faculty is not their increasing numbers but rather "the institutional neglect of this critical mass" (p. 92). Using one institution's response to the growing population of part-time faculty, she describes how policies and practices can be implemented to integrate this group into the campus culture better. In particular, she suggests that the following areas need to be examined: institutional recruitment, selection, and hiring practices of part-time faculty; appointment and reappointment provisions; working conditions; orientation and integration into the institutional culture, policies, practices, and department processes; professional development opportunities; work evaluation; and equitable versus equal pay.

Roueche, J. E., Roueche, S. D., and Milliron, M. D. "Identifying the Strangers: Exploring Part-Time Faculty Integration in American Community Colleges." *Community College Review,* 1996, 23(4), 33–48. This article summarizes the qualitative phase of a mixed-methods study concerning how to improve the use of part-time faculty. Using an organizational identification theoretical framework based on the "dynamic interaction between individuals and the organization during socialization, communication, and decision-making" (p. 35), the authors develop a part-time faculty integration model to inform their analysis. Their aim is to explore strategies that enable part-time faculty to "feel less like strangers and more like valuable organizational players" (p. 34) and become better integrated into the organizational cultures of community colleges. Results indicate that efforts by college administrators to "aggressively and systemically" integrate part-time faculty are minimal. Nevertheless, findings from the colleges profiled do suggest that part-time faculty integration is possible and the authors offer strategies and recommendations for accomplishing this.

What Is Significant About Part-Time Faculty?

With greater numbers of part-time faculty teaching in community colleges, an important area of inquiry to examine is their effectiveness and influence as instructors and as a community college constituent group. What effects might they have on pedagogy, retention, and learning outcomes? How might they affect the culture of community colleges? The following works begin to address these questions.

Nutting, M. M. "Part-Time Faculty: Why Should We Care?" In E. Benjamin (ed.), *Exploring the Role of Contingent Instructional Staff in Undergraduate Learning*. New Directions for Higher Education, no. 123. San Francisco: Jossey-Bass, 2003. In this chapter, Nutting discusses from a seemingly anecdotal rather than empirical perspective the positive and negative effects that part-time faculty have on students, faculty, staff, administrators, and institutions. Drawing from her own experience teaching at a community college in Seattle, she argues that part-time faculty have "assumed critical roles, if not clear identities" (p. 33), outlines at length the obstacles facing part-time faculty, and offers some remedies to the adverse effects she believes part-time instruction can have on campuses.

Keim, M. C., and Biletzky, P. E. "Teaching Methods Used by Part-Time Community College Faculty." *Community College Journal of Research and Practice,* 1999, 23(8), 727–737. The purpose of this study was to determine the teaching methods of typical part-time community college instructors. Using a Likert scale to indicate how often instructors used twenty-one different teaching methods and practices, the authors surveyed 240 part-time faculty teaching transfer courses at four community colleges in southern Illinois. With a 58 percent response rate, findings indicate that part-time faculty tend to employ traditional teaching methods, thereby neglecting newer teaching strategies. The most common pedagogies were lecture, class discussion, written feedback, and methods to engage critical thinking. Least popular were slides, field trips, audiotapes, and guest lecturers. Further statistical analyses found that faculty who had participated in professional development were more likely to use small group discussions, demonstrations, and activities to promote critical thinking.

Jacoby, D. "Effects of Part-Time Faculty Employment on Community College Graduation Rates." *Journal of Higher Education,* 2006, 77(6), 1081–1103. Using data from the Integrated Postsecondary Education Data

Systems (IPEDS), Jacoby employs multiple regression analysis to test whether graduation rates at public community colleges vary as schools increase their reliance on part-time faculty. Without a single, uniform measure of community college graduation rates, identical analyses are performed using three dependent variables of community college performance: IPEDS graduation rate, the net graduation rate, and the overall degree ratio. The author is careful to note the limitations of the data source, including most notably the omission of variables that measure student ability and motivation. The primary finding from this study is that increases in the ratio of part-time faculty at community colleges have a highly significant and negative impact on graduation rates. Based on these results, Jacoby suggests that schools aiming to stretch their instructional dollars by increasing their part-time faculty ratio will find it counterproductive if they are held accountable for higher graduation rates.

Burgess, L. A., and Samuels, C. "Impact of Full-Time Versus Part-Time Instructor Status on College Student Retention and Academic Performance in Sequential Courses." *Community College Journal of Research and Practice,* 1999, 23(5), 487–498. In any two-course sequence, the four possible instructor status combinations are full-time and full-time, part-time and part-time, full-time and part-time, and part-time and full-time. The main focus of this study was to examine the impact of instructor status on student academic performance and retention in sequential courses. The dependent variables measuring student academic performance and retention were the number of students achieving a grade of C or better and the number of students completing the courses. Drawing on data from a large, urban multicampus community college district, the authors examine the student grades and course completion rates of four two-course sequences of developmental math, regular math, and regular English courses. Results from chi-square tests generally suggest that in sequential courses, "part-time instructors under prepare their students for subsequent courses taught by full-time instructors" (p. 498). Correspondingly, the data indicate that students in sequential courses whose first course is taught by a full-time instructor are better prepared for their second course, whether it is taught by a full-time or part-time instructor.

Wagoner, R. L., Metcalfe, A. S., and Olaore, I. "Fiscal Reality and Academic Quality: Part-Time Faculty and the Challenge to Organizational Culture at Community Colleges." *Community College Journal of Research and Practice,* 2004, 29(1), 25–44. This qualitative case study explores academic administrators' policies, opinions, and practices concerning part-time faculty to better understand how they contribute to the academic climate. Findings derive from semistructured interviews with high-level administrators at one multicampus community college. The authors examine how the use of part-time faculty illuminates the traditional, service, hierarchical, and business cultures (Levin, 1997) of community colleges and its organizational dynamics. In analyzing the responses, the authors consider how the four cultures demonstrate integration, differentiation, and ambiguity. They suggest that community colleges' use of part-time faculty, including the willingness to exploit the part-time labor market, is attuned with the general labor trends of globalization on the rise at community college campuses.

Levin, J. "Neo-Liberal Policies and Community College Faculty Work." In J. Smart and W. Tierney (eds.), *Handbook of Higher Education*. Norwell, Mass.: Kluwer, 2007. In this chapter, Levin localizes the paradigms of globalization, neoliberalism, and corporatism to the faculty labor force at community colleges. He explores the notion of community colleges as "new world colleges" and considers how community colleges have been reinstitutionalized into a newer form that is compatible with a twenty-first-century world order. Regarding part-time faculty in particular, he states that despite their lower rank on the professional labor hierarchy, they are nevertheless critical to the "strategic plans of modern organizations" (p. 479). However, they are at constant risk of exploitation, subject to the whims and controls of managerialism and economic efficiency.

What Is the Future of Part-Time Faculty?

Research and anecdotal evidence suggest that the rising tide of part-time faculty at community colleges is unlikely to recede. Some of the studies annotated here point to the negative effects of part-time faculty on graduation and course retention, but a more thorough reading of those studies and the literature they review indicates that the evidence is at best inconclusive. Part-time faculty integration into campus cultures, however, is generally agreed to be of paramount importance for ensuring their success. Further research on part-time faculty is needed to fully capture their importance and influence on students and institutions. As community colleges are recharacterized into new world colleges, it will be imperative to understand how the dynamics, demographics, and effects of part-time faculty inform the changes.

References

Cataldi, E. F., Fahimi, M., Bradburn, E. M., and Zimbler, L. *2004 National Study of Post-Secondary Faculty Report on Faculty and Instructional Staff*. Washington, D.C.: U.S. Department of Education, 2005.
Levin, J. "The Cultures of the Community College." Paper presented at the annual meeting of the Association for the Study of Higher Education, Albuquerque, N.M., Nov. 1997.

AMY LIU *is a doctoral student in higher education at the University of California, Los Angeles.*

NEW DIRECTIONS FOR COMMUNITY COLLEGES • DOI: 10.1002/cc

INDEX

89

and industry? Providing transfer education? Workforce training and continuing education? This volume's chapters will stimulate thinking and discussion among policy-makers, leaders, scholars, and educators.
ISBN: 0-7879-9575-4

CC135   **Pathways To and From the Community College**
Debra D. Bragg, Elisabeth A. Barnett
Examines local, state, and federal programs to help underserved students enter and succeed in college. Focuses on "academic pathways," boundary-spanning curricula, instructional strategies, and organizational structures to link high schools with two- and four-year colleges. The academic pathways support students during transitions and can be alternate routes to educational attainment. Topics include dual enrollment, dual credit, early and middle college high schools, plus career and technical education pathways and emerging models.
ISBN: 0-7879-9422-7

CC134   **Benchmarking: An Essential Tool for Assessment, Improvement, and Accountability**
Jeffrey A. Seybert
Comparing your institution's performance to that of its peers is a critical part of assessing institutional effectiveness and student learning outcomes. Two-year colleges now have access to national data collection and reporting consortia to identify and benchmark with peer schools. This volume describes the costs and benefits of benchmarking, the newly available community college data, and how your institution can use it for assessment and improvement.
ISBN: 0-7879-8758-1

CC133   **Latino Educational Opportunity**
Catherine L. Horn, Stella M. Flores, Gary Orfield
Latinos enroll at community colleges at rates higher than any other racial or ethnic group. Many factors influence Latino education—immigration policy, language, academic opportunity, family—and, despite research, the influence of these factors remains confounding. This issue explains the ways and extent to which community colleges can provide Latino students with access and opportunity.
ISBN: 0-7879-8624-0

CC132   **Sustaining Financial Support for Community Colleges**
Stephen G. Katsinas, James C. Palmer
Describes institutional approaches for securing adequate funding in an era of recurrent recessions, legislator reluctance to raise taxes, and intense competition for scarce resources. Chapter authors give guidelines for fundraising, corporate partnerships, grants for workforce development, mill levy elections, realigning budget priorities, and the key skills that today's community college presidents need.
ISBN: 0-7879-8364-0

CC131   **Community College Student Affairs: What Really Matters**
Steven R. Helfgot, Marguerite M. Culp
Uses the results of a national survey to identify the major challenges and opportunities for student affairs practitioners in community colleges, and describes the most effective strategies for meeting challenges. Chapters discuss core values, cultures of evidence, faculty partnerships, career counseling, and support for underrepresented populations, plus assessment tools and best practices in student affairs.
ISBN: 0-7879-8332-2

CC130   Critical Thinking: Unfinished Business
Christine M. McMahon
With a few exceptions, critical thinking is not being effectively taught or
even correctly understood in higher education. This volume advocates for
professional development in critical thinking to engage all members of the
campus community. It presents blueprints for such development, plus
practical case studies from campuses already doing it. Also covers classroom
assignments, solutions to resistance, and program assessment.
ISBN: 0-7879-8185-0

CC129   Responding to the Challenges of Developmental Education
Carol A. Kozeracki
Approximately 40 percent of incoming community college students enroll in
developmental math, English, or reading courses. Despite the availability of
popular models for teaching these classes, community colleges continue to
struggle with effectively educating underprepared students, who have a wide
variety of backgrounds. This volume discusses the dangers of isolating
developmental education from the broader college; provides examples of
successful programs; offers recommendations adaptable to different
campuses; and identifies areas for future research.
ISBN: 0-7879-8050-1

CC128   From Distance Education to E-Learning: Lessons Along the Way
Beverly L. Bower, Kimberly P. Hardy
Correspondence, telecourses, and now e-learning: distance education
continues to grow and change. This volume's authors examine what
community colleges must do to make distance education successful,
including meeting technology challenges, containing costs, developing
campuswide systems, teaching effectively, balancing faculty workloads,
managing student services, and redesigning courses for online learning.
Includes case studies from colleges, plus state and regional policy
perspectives.
ISBN: 0-7879-7927-9

CC127   Serving Minority Populations
Berta Vigil Laden
Focuses on how colleges with emerging majority enrollments of African
American, Hispanic, American Indian, Asian American and Pacific Islander,
and other ethnically diverse students are responding to the needs—
academic, financial, and cultural—of their increasingly diverse student
populations. Discusses partnerships with universities, businesses,
foundations, and professional associations that can increase access,
retention, and overall academic success for students of color. Covers best
practices from Minority-Serving Institutions, and offers examples for
mainstream community colleges.
ISBN: 0-7879-7790-X

**CC126   Developing and Implementing Assessment of Student Learning
Outcomes**
Andreea M. Serban, Jack Friedlander
Colleges are under increasing pressure to produce evidence of student
learning, but most assessment research focuses on four-year colleges. This
volume is designed for practitioners looking for models that community
colleges can apply to measuring student learning outcomes at the classroom,
course, program, and institutional levels to satisfy legislative and
accreditation requirements.
ISBN: 0-7879-7687-3

CC125 **Legal Issues in the Community College**
Robert C. Cloud
Community colleges must be prepared for lawsuits, federal statutes, court
rulings, union negotiations, and other legal issues that could affect
institutional stability and effectiveness. This volume provides leaders with
information about board relations, tenure and employment, student rights
and safety, disability law, risk management, copyright and technology
issues, and more.
ISBN: 0-7879-7482-X

NEW DIRECTIONS FOR COMMUNITY COLLEGES
Order Form
SUBSCRIPTIONS AND SINGLE ISSUES

DISCOUNTED BACK ISSUES:

Use this form to receive **20% off** all back issues of New Directions for Community Colleges. All single issues are priced at **$23.20** (normally $29.00).

TITLE	ISSUE NO.	ISBN
_____	_____	_____
_____	_____	_____
_____	_____	_____

Call 888-378-2537 or see mailing instructions below. When calling, mention the promotional code JB7ND to receive your discount.

SUBSCRIPTIONS: (1 year, 4 issues)

☐ New Order   ☐ Renewal

U.S.	☐ Individual: $80	☐ Institutional: $195
Canada/Mexico	☐ Individual: $80	☐ Institutional: $235
All Others	☐ Individual: $104	☐ Institutional: $269

Call 888-378-2537 or see mailing and pricing instructions below. Online subscriptions are available at www.interscience.wiley.com.

Copy or detach page and send to:
John Wiley & Sons, Journals Dept, 5th Floor
989 Market Street, San Francisco, CA 94103-1741

Order Form can also be faxed to: 888-481-2665

Issue/Subscription Amount: $ _____

Shipping Amount: $ _____

(for single issues only—subscription prices include shipping)

Total Amount: $ _____

SHIPPING CHARGES:		
SURFACE	Domestic	Canadian
First Item	$5.00	$6.00
Each Add'l Item	$3.00	$1.50

(No sales tax for U.S. subscriptions. Canadian residents, add GST for subscription orders. Individual rate subscriptions must be paid by personal check or credit card. Individual rate subscriptions may not be resold as library copies.)

☐ Payment enclosed (U.S. check or money order only. All payments must be in U.S. dollars.)

☐ VISA ☐ MC ☐ Amex # _____ Exp. Date_____

Card Holder Name _____ Card Issue # _____

Signature_____ Day Phone _____

☐ Bill Me (U.S. institutional orders only. Purchase order required.)

Purchase order # _____

Federal Tax ID13559302   GST 89102 8052

Name_____

Address _____

Phone _____ E-mail _____

**NEW DIRECTIONS FOR COMMUNITY COLLEGES
IS NOW AVAILABLE ONLINE AT WILEY INTERSCIENCE**

What is Wiley InterScience?

Wiley InterScience is the dynamic online content service from John Wiley & Sons delivering the full text of over 300 leading scientific, technical, medical, and professional journals, plus major reference works, the acclaimed *Current Protocols* laboratory manuals, and even the full text of select Wiley print books online.

What are some special features of Wiley InterScience?

Wiley InterScience Alerts is a service that delivers table of contents via e-mail for any journal available on Wiley InterScience as soon as a new issue is published online.
Early View is Wiley's exclusive service presenting individual articles online as soon as they are ready, even before the release of the compiled print issue. These articles are complete, peer-reviewed, and citable.
CrossRef is the innovative multi-publisher reference linking system enabling readers to move seamlessly from a reference in a journal article to the cited publication, typically located on a different server and published by a different publisher.

How can I access Wiley InterScience?

Visit http://www.interscience.wiley.com

Guest Users can browse Wiley InterScience for unrestricted access to journal Tables of Contents and Article Abstracts, or use the powerful search engine.
Registered Users are provided with a *Personal Home Page* to store and manage customized alerts, searches, and links to favorite journals and articles. Additionally, Registered Users can view free Online Sample Issues and preview selected material from major reference works.
Licensed Customers are entitled to access full-text journal articles in PDF, with select journals also offering full-text HTML.

How do I become an Authorized User?

Authorized Users are individuals authorized by a paying Customer to have access to the journals in Wiley InterScience. For example, a university that subscribes to Wiley journals is considered to be the Customer. Faculty, staff and students authorized by the university to have access to those journals in Wiley InterScience are Authorized Users. Users should contact their Library for information on which Wiley journals they have access to in Wiley InterScience.

ASK YOUR INSTITUTION ABOUT WILEY INTERSCIENCE TODAY!

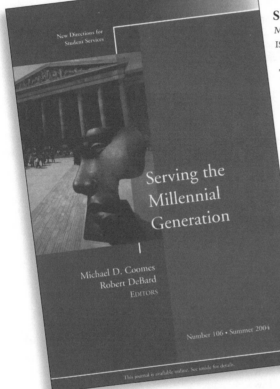

<table>
<tr><td colspan="2">UNITED STATES POSTAL SERVICE</td><td colspan="2">Statement of Ownership, Management, and Circulation
(All Periodicals Publications Except Requester Publications)</td></tr>
</table>

1. Publication Title	2. Publication Number		3. Filing Date
New Directions for Community Colleges	0 1 9 4 _ 3 0 8 1		10/1/2007

4. Issue Frequency	5. Number of Issues Published Annually	6. Annual Subscription Price
Quarterly	4	$209

7. Complete Mailing Address of Known Office of Publication (Not printer) (Street, city, county, state, and ZIP+4®)	Contact Person
Wiley Subscriptions Services, Inc. at Jossey-Bass, 989 Market St., San Francisco, CA 94103	Joe Schuman
	Telephone (Include area code) 415-782-3232

8. Complete Mailing Address of Headquarters or General Business Office of Publisher (Not printer)

Wiley Subscriptions Services, Inc., 111 River Street, Hoboken, NJ 07030

9. Full Names and Complete Mailing Addresses of Publisher, Editor, and Managing Editor (Do not leave blank)

Publisher (Name and complete mailing address)

Wiley Subscriptions Services, Inc., A Wiley Company at San Francisco, 989 Market St., San Francisco, CA 94103-1741

Editor (Name and complete mailing address)

Arthur M. Cohen, Eric Clearinghouse for Community Colleges, 3051 Moore Hall, Box 95121, Los Angeles, CA 90095

Managing Editor (Name and complete mailing address)

None

10. Owner (Do not leave blank. If the publication is owned by a corporation, give the name and address of the corporation immediately followed by the names and addresses of all stockholders owning or holding 1 percent or more of the total amount of stock. If not owned by a corporation, give the names and addresses of the individual owners. If owned by a partnership or other unincorporated firm, give its name and address as well as those of each individual owner. If the publication is published by a nonprofit organization, give its name and address.)

Full Name	Complete Mailing Address
Wiley Subscriptions Services	111 River Street, Hoboken, NJ
(see attached list)	

11. Known Bondholders, Mortgagees, and Other Security Holders Owning or Holding 1 Percent or More of Total Amount of Bonds, Mortgages, or Other Securities. If none, check box ▸ ☑ None

Full Name	Complete Mailing Address

12. Tax Status (For completion by nonprofit organizations authorized to mail at nonprofit rates) (Check one)
The purpose, function, and nonprofit status of this organization and the exempt status for federal income tax purposes:
☐ Has Not Changed During Preceding 12 Months
☐ Has Changed During Preceding 12 Months (Publisher must submit explanation of change with this statement)

13. Publication Title	14. Issue Date for Circulation Data
New Directions for Community Colleges	Summer 2007

15. Extent and Nature of Circulation		Average No. Copies Each Issue During Preceding 12 Months	No. Copies of Single Issue Published Nearest to Filing Date
a. Total Number of Copies (Net press run)		1589	1589
b. Paid Circulation (By Mail and Outside the Mail)	(1) Mailed Outside-County Paid Subscriptions Stated on PS Form 3541(Include paid distribution above nominal rate, advertiser's proof copies, and exchange copies)	662	674
	(2) Mailed In-County Paid Subscriptions Stated on PS Form 3541 (Include paid distribution above nominal rate, advertiser's proof copies, and exchange copies)	0	0
	(3) Paid Distribution Outside the Mails Including Sales Through Dealers and Carriers, Street Vendors, Counter Sales, and Other Paid Distribution Outside USPS®	0	0
	(4) Paid Distribution by Other Classes of Mail Through the USPS (e.g. First-Class Mail®)		0
c. Total Paid Distribution (Sum of 15b (1), (2),(3), and (4))		662	674
d. Free or Nominal Rate Distribution (By Mail and Outside the Mail)	(1) Free or Nominal Rate Outside-County Copies Iincluded on PS Form 3541	145	146
	(2) Free or Nominal Rate In-County Copies Included on PS Form 3541	0	0
	(3) Free or Nominal Rate Copies Mailed at Other Classes Through the USPS (e.g. First-Class Mail)	0	0
	(4) Free or Nominal Rate Distribution Outside the Mail (Carriers or other means)	0	0
e. Total Free or Nominal Rate Distribution (Sum of 15d (1), (2), (3) and (4)		145	146
f. Total Distribution (Sum of 15c and 15e) ▸		807	820
g. Copies not Distributed (See Instructions to Publishers #4 (page #3)) ▸		782	769
h. Total (Sum of 15f and g) ▸		1589	1589
i. Percent Paid (15c divided by 15f times 100) ▸		82%	82%

16. Publication of Statement of Ownership
☐ If the publication is a general publication, publication of this statement is required. Will be printed in the WINTER 2007 issue of this publication.
☐ Publication not required.

17. Signature and Title of Editor, Publisher, Business Manager, or Owner	Date
Susan E. Lewis, VP & Publisher - Periodicals	10/1/2007

I certify that all information furnished on this form is true and complete. I understand that anyone who furnishes false or misleading information on this form or who omits material or information requested on the form may be subject to criminal sanctions (including fines and imprisonment) and/or civil sanctions (including civil penalties).